917.4
H
N480257   v.1

Library of Congress
Cataloging in Publication Data

Hechtlinger, Adelaide.
*The Pelican guide to historic homes and sites of
Revolutionary America.*

Includes index.
CONTENTS: v. 1 New England.
1. Historic buildings—United States—Guide-books
2. United States—Description and travel—1960-   —
Guide-books. I. Title.
E159.H42   917.4'04'4   76-20434
ISBN 0-88289-090-5

3953

Manufactured in the United States of America

Published by Pelican Publishing Company, Inc.
630 Burmaster Street, Gretna, Louisiana 70053

Contents

ACKNOWLEDGMENTS

I would like to thank all those persons, too numerous to name individually, who were kind enough to help me with information concerning the various landmarks and sites with which they are connected. Without their kind assistance, this book could not have been put together.

Maine

HISTORY

The first known claim by the English to the territory now known as Maine was made near Weymouth in 1605. Not until John Smith's expedition of 1614 was the area explored, mapped, and named New England.

The first colony in this northern land was the Popham settlement at the mouth of the Kennebec River, which was begun in 1607 and abandoned in 1608. The earliest permanent settlement was York, founded in 1624, followed by Scarborough and Falmouth, now Portland, in the early 1630s.

In 1677, Massachusetts purchased the province of Maine from the heirs of Ferdinando Gorgas, one of the first proprietors. With the charter of 1691, Maine was extended to the St. Croix River and made part of Massachusetts. However, there was a small, poorly defended populace there between 1675 and 1763. The British controlled the territory until the American Revolution, at which time Portland was burned for its resistance. Maine was also the scene of the first naval battle of the war, involving the capture of the British cutter *Margaretta,* which occurred in Machias Bay.

AUGUSTA

A colony was founded here in 1628. Fur and pelt trading with the Indians was so profitable that the Pilgrims of Augusta were able to repay the London loans which had made the Plymouth adventure possible. John Alden and Captain Miles Standish were among the original settlers. In 1754, Fort Western was erected on the east bank of the Kennebec River to protect the colony.

FORT WESTERN: Bowman and Cony streets.

This fort, built in 1754, is an excellent example of early fortifications. It also was the starting point for Benedict Arnold's expedition against Quebec in 1775. Fort Western now houses a collection of Early Americana.

Open: Mid-May to mid-September, weekdays, 9 to 5; guided tours only.
Admission: Nominal fee charged.

CASTINE

FORT GEORGE

The French built the first fort at Castine in 1613 but the first permanent settlement was made by the English in 1760. The British occupied the town during the Revolution and built Fort George which passed into American hands in 1783. The earthworks and protective moat are still visible.
Open: Memorial Day through Labor Day, daily, 10 to 6.
Admission: Free.

DAMARISCOTTA

CHAPMAN-HALL HOUSE

This house, built in 1754, has been partially restored and includes a collection of eighteenth-century crafts, farming and ship-building tools, as well as typical furnishings of the day.
Open: June 15 to September 15, 1 to 5; closed Mondays.
Admission: Nominal fee charged.

HARPSWELL CENTER

HARPSWELL MEETINGHOUSE: Me. 1239, 9 miles south of Brunswick.
This simple, clapboard, two-storied frame church was erected in 1757-59 probably by Elisha Eaton, a carpenter and son of the first pastor. The church interior measures about 30 by 40 feet. The main structure contains one large room with galleries at the second floor level extending around three sides. The building was used both as a church and, beginning in 1744, for town meetings.

KENNEBUNK

Kennebunk, first settled about 1650, was once a leading ship-building town. Although there are still a number of early houses in town dating from 1752 to 1826, they are privately owned and can only be enjoyed from the outside.

BRICK STORE: 117 Maine Street.

At this museum, one can obtain a map that points out the locations of the town's historic houses.

FIRST PARISH CHURCH (Unitarian)

This church was built about 1772. The fine steeple contains a bell cast by Paul Revere and hung there in 1804.

KITTERY

Kittery, incorporated in 1647, became an important shipbuilding, shipping, and lumbering town. The *Ranger*, first ship to fly the Stars and Stripes, was launched here May 10, 1777.

OLD CHURCH (First Congregational)

This church was built in 1730.

Open: Summer, daily.

Admission: Free.

LADY PEPPERELL HOUSE: State 103, 2½ miles east of U.S. 1.

This mansion was built by the widow of Sir William Pepperell as a monument to her late husband. She was the daughter of Judge Grove Hirst, a wealthy Boston merchant, and a granddaughter of Judge Samuel Sewall. Sir William Pepperell had been commander of American land forces at the siege and capture of Louisberg, off Nova Scotia. He was made a baronet because of his invaluable services to the British in their troubles with the French and the Indians. Sir Pepperell also was known as one of the wealthiest men in the Colonies. He died in 1759, and his widow built the house in 1760 where she lived until 1789, the time of her death. Even after the Revolution, she insisted upon being addressed by her title.

The house is quite as aristocratic as those manor houses of the Tidewater South, but is built of wood instead of brick. The house has a hipped roof which is free of dormers. Chippendale, Hepplewhite, Sheraton, and Duncan Phyfe furniture add charm to the house as do its fine glass, china, mirrors, and paintings.

Open: Mid-June to mid-September, Tuesday through Saturday, 11 to 4.

Admission: Nominal fee charged.

MACHIAS

Machias, founded in 1763, is the oldest town east of the Penobscot River. It was in Machias Bay that one of the earliest naval engagements was fought, when colonists captured the English warship *Margaretta* in June of 1775.

BURNHAM TAVERN: Main and Free streets.

The tavern dates back to 1770 and contains many articles of the era. The first owner placed slips of paper beneath each of the four cornerstones reading "Hospitality," "Cheer," "Hope," and "Courage." They are still there.

Open: June through August, Tuesdays, Wednesdays, and Thursdays, 2 to 5 or by appointment.

Admission: Adults, nominal fee charged; children under 12, free.

Shaker Museum, Exterior

POLAND SPRING

SHAKER MUSEUM: Sabbathday Lake on State 26.

This cooperative community dates from 1782. The museum houses a fine display of inventions, handicrafts, and furniture as made by the Shakers.

Open: Memorial Day to September 30, Tuesday through Saturday and holidays, 10 to 4:30.

Admission: Adults, nominal fee charged; children under 6, free. Walking tour—nominal fee charged.

Shaker Museum, Interior

PORTLAND

Portland was destroyed three times—once by Indians, once by the French and Indians, and the third time by a British fleet in 1775.

WADSWORTH-LONGFELLOW HOUSE: 487 Congress Street.

This house, constructed in 1785, was the first brick building in Portland. It was built by the grandfather of Henry Wadsworth Longfellow, who lived there as a child. The home still contains furniture and personal property of the Longfellow and Wadsworth families.

Open: Mid-June to mid-October, Monday through Saturday, 9:30 to 4:30.

Admission: Nominal fee charged; guide service available.

STROUDWATER

TATE HOUSE: 1270 Broad Street, 3 miles west of Portland. This house dates back to 1755. When the British sent a small naval force to Casco Bay and destroyed Falmouth (now Portland), only a handful of notable houses built before the Revolution survived. Tate House survived because it was outside the old town of Falmouth and because it had been built by George Tate, mast agent for the British navy, whose job it was to secure the tallest, soundest trees available; each tree over a certain circumference was marked with an arrowhead to indicate that it belonged to the king.

Open: July to mid-September, daily except Mondays 11 to 5, Sundays 1:30 to 4.

Admission: Nominal fee charged.

SOUTH BERWICK

HAMILTON HOUSE: 1½ miles south of South Berwick, off State 91 and 236.

Colonel Jonathan Hamilton became rich through retail trade, as he said, "selling salt-fish, molasses, rum, sugar and tea in exchange for wood, timber, poultry, butter and eggs." It was his ambition to build the finest house in Berwick. Begun in 1785, his mansion built on the high bluff overlooking the Piscataqua River was completed in 1788.

Colonel Hamilton built his house at a time when Maine shipping fortunes were recovering from the low state that they had been in throughout the Revolution. His trade with the West Indies had resumed. At about the time that he moved into his new mansion, Hamilton was the leading citizen of Old Berwick.

From the windows of the drawing room he could see his ships come around the bend. To the north and east lay the stables and office buildings, slave quarters, spinning house, and high, green fields.

John Paul Jones was a frequent visitor to Hamilton's house, which was also the scene of Sarah Orne Jewett's book *The Tory Lover*. The house features lovely gardens and eighteenth-century furnishings.

Open: June through September, Wednesday through Saturday, 1 to 5; closed holidays.

Admission: Nominal fee charged.

SARAH ORNE JEWETT HOUSE: Main and Portland streets.

This house was built in 1774 by Miss Jewett's grandfather and passed on to her father before she inherited it. The house has a woman's touch that is most notable in the various rooms as all the furnishings are hers. One of the wallpapers was intended for a French colonial governor in Portsmouth, but somehow the paper got here instead. The house is now a museum with an interesting collection of period furnishings.

Open: June through September, Wednesday through Saturday, 1 to 5; closed holidays.

Admission: Nominal fee charged.

THOMASTON

The first known claim by an Englishman of New England soil was made here in 1605, when Captain George Weymouth planted a cross on Allen's Island, off the mouth of St. George's River. In 1630 a post for trading with the Indians was established, and in 1736 Thomaston was founded. A number of fine colonial houses may yet be viewed throughout the town.

MONTPELIER: Route 1, 1 mile north of town.

This house was originally the Henry Knox House, built in 1795 to celebrate the hero of the Battle of Bunker Hill and the secretary of war in Washington's first cabinet. The house has eighteen rooms and all are furnished with antiques, many of them saved when the original house burned down.

Open: May 30 to October 31, daily, 10 to 6.

Admission: Nominal fee charged.

WINSLOW

FORT HALIFAX: U.S. 201.

Fort Halifax was erected in 1754 on a site selected by Governor William Shirley. It contains the oldest surviving example in the United States of a log blockhouse, a defensive structure that was used by explorers, fur traders, and settlers along the early American frontier.

A blockhouse can be constructed of stone, brick, or adobe as well as of logs. It was a very effective defense on the frontier, as it usually was able to repel any enemy force not equipped with artillery.

The blockhouse is the only extant structure of Fort Halifax, which was originally a square enclosed by a log stockade with blockhouses at the southwest and northeast corners.

YORK

JEFFERDS' TAVERN: Faces the village graveyard.

This ancient inn was built by Captain Samuel Jefferd in 1750. Jefferds' Tavern stood on the King's highway in the nearby township of Wells. This tavern not only served stagecoach travelers with refreshment on the run between York and Kennebunk, but was also a neighborhood "Publick House." There are retiring rooms for women and children on the second floor.

Open: Memorial Day through September 15, Monday through Saturday 9:30 to 5:30, Sundays 1:30 to 5:30.

Admission: Nominal fee charged.

FIRST PARISH CONGREGATIONAL CHURCH: Village Green.

This church was erected in 1747. The first church in York was an Anglican chapel built prior to 1636, the first church built in the English colonies after the one at Jamestown, Virginia.

EMERSON-WILCOX HOUSE

This house was built in 1740 on church land later leased for 999 years. The house has been a tavern, post office, and private residence. It now contains rooms furnished in period style.

Open: June through September, Monday through Saturday 9:30 to 5, Sundays 1:30 to 5.

Admission: Nominal fee charged.

OLD SCHOOL HOUSE: Faces graveyard.

The first written record of any schoolmaster in York appears in 1676. There was no schoolhouse at that time, but the children were taught in the schoolmaster's home. In 1711, it was decided that children had to be 5 years of age to attend school and should attend seven hours daily. They were taught reading, writing, and cyphering.

This school was built in 1745. It contains figures dressed in period costumes, as well as such former teaching materials as the hornbook.

Open: June 15 to September 14, Monday through Saturday 9:30 to 5:30, Sundays 1:30 to 5:30.

Admission: Free.

ELIZABETH PERKINS HOUSE: South Side Road at Sewall's Bridge.

This house was constructed about 1730 and was occupied by the Perkins family as a summer residence until the last Miss Perkins died in 1952. The central part of the house, now the dining room, and its chimney were probably all there was to the original small cottage. The beams are of white oak. This colonial house displays fine Victorian furnishings.

Open: June 15 to September 15, Monday through Saturday 9:30 to 5:30, Sundays 1:30 to 5:30.

Admission: Nominal fee charged.

JOHN HANCOCK WAREHOUSE: On the York River.

This warehouse is the only colonial commercial building standing in York, and was once owned by John Hancock. It now features exhibits of colonial tools and antique models.

Open: June 15 to September 15, Monday through Saturday 9:30 to 5:30, Sundays 1:30 to 5:30.

Admission: Free.

OLD GAOL: 4 Lindsay Road.

This is one of the oldest public buildings in New England. York was established in 1624 by the Plymouth Company. In 1641, it formed a government and adopted a city charter, and in 1652 reorganized into a town. Many public buildings were then constructed such as the gaol, built of stone in 1652, which is the oldest extant building in York.

On October 6, 1719, the Massachusetts Court of General Sessions ordered, "That a prison of thirty foot long eighteen foot wide & eight foot tall be built with Stone or brick in the town of York." The court also requested that "The old prison and the land it stands on Shall be disposed of & a meetting house in se York to build the new Prison upon."

The original prisoners' cells may be seen in the old part of the structure. The gaol is now a museum, and contains various colonial and Indian relics.

Open: June through September, weekdays 9:30 to 5, Sundays 1:30 to 5.

Admission: Nominal fee charged.

McINTIRE GARRISON HOUSE: Me. 91 about 5 miles west of York.

This house, built either in 1690 or 1707, is representative of the log architecture that was used in New England during the seventeenth century as a defense against Indians. If built in 1690, as some claim, it is the oldest log structure in the United States. Garrisons or fortified houses with thick protective walls were built in almost all New England towns, and they were particularly common in the frontier towns of Maine and New Hampshire.

In time of peace, the garrisons were used as one-family dwellings. Clapboard and shingle siding and sash windows were added to the McIntire Garrison House in the eighteenth century, but in 1909 the building was restored to its earlier appearance.

Open: June through September, weekdays 9:30 to 5, Sundays 1:30 to 5.

Admission: Nominal fee charged.

Vermont

HISTORY

The first Vermont settlement, Fort Drummer, was made in 1724 on a site near the present town of Brattleboro. From 1744 to 1759 there was incessant fighting in the area until the French abandoned their New England claims. Meanwhile, part of the state was claimed by New York and part by New Hampshire. An appeal to the British Crown was decided in favor of New York, who attempted to force the settlers to repurchase their holdings from Albany.

To protect the settlers, several local militia banded together in 1770 and, led by Ethan Allen and Remember Baker, they gained fame as the Green Mountain Boys. This group was active in the American Revolution and instrumental in the capture of Fort Ticonderoga. In 1777 they were among the Americans routed at Hubbardton, and they fought under Seth Warner in the Battle of Bennington.

In 1777, Vermont declared its independence and became a separate state. In 1791 it was admitted to the United States as the fourteenth state.

BENNINGTON

On August 16, 1777, the Battle of Bennington was fought, the Americans under General John Stark defeating a British expedition sent by Burgoyne. Two separate forces of British, Hessian, Loyalist, and Indian troops sent to seize the military stores of the Continental Army were repulsed.

TOPPING TAVERN MUSEUM: Nearby Shaftsbury.
This late eighteenth-century stagecoach tavern features period furniture, cooking implements, and other household items.
Open: May 1 to October 31, Tuesday through Saturday and holidays 10 to 5, Sundays 1 to 5.

OLD FIRST CHURCH (Congregational): Monument Avenue in Old Bennington Village.

This church, dating back to 1762, is the oldest in Vermont although this building dates back to 1805.

Open: Late May to late October, weekdays 9 to 5; Sundays 1 to 5.

Admission: Donations.

CASTLETON

HUBBARDTON BATTLEFIELD AND MUSEUM: East Hubbardton, 7 miles north of U.S. 4.

This is the site of the only battle fought on Vermont soil. Colonels Seth Warner and Ebenezer Francis, in charge of the rear guard of the American forces retreating after the fall of Fort Ticonderoga, remained overnight at Hubbardton without taking proper security measures. As a result, the British attacked very early in the following morning, July 7, 1777, and there was a brief but severe fight. Colonel Francis was killed,

Hubbardton Monument

and the Americans scattered with instructions to reassemble at Manchester. The British advance was delayed but the cost was exorbitant.

Open: Memorial Day to mid-October, Monday through Saturday 8 to 4, Sundays 9 to 5.

Admission: Adults, nominal fee charged; children under 16, free.

SHELBURNE

SHELBURNE MUSEUM: Center on U.S. 7, 7 miles south of Burlington.

This outdoor museum of early New England life is composed of thirty-five buildings, many of which were moved to the site from other areas. Many early crafts are represented and demonstrated.

Open: May 15 to October 15, daily, 9 to 5.

Admission: Fee charged; second consecutive visit, students free; children under 6 free at all times.

Dorset House

Covered Bridge

General Store

WINDSOR

OLD CONSTITUTION HOUSE: 16 North Main Street. This tavern was built in 1768 which makes it one of the earliest taverns in the state. The constitution of Vermont was drawn up and signed here in 1777, while the first session of the legislature met here. The building is now a museum, furnished with antiques.

Open: Mid-May to mid-October, daily, 10 to 5.
Admission: Free.

New Hampshire

HISTORY

The first explorer of the territory now known as New Hampshire was an Englishman named Martin Fring, who came to the area in 1603. Fring was followed in 1605 by Samuel de Champlain and in 1614 by John Smith. The first Englishmen to settle in this region landed in 1623 on the rocky coast at Odiorne's Point. These colonists established settlements in Rye, Portsmouth, Exeter, and Hampton, which for many years were the only towns in the state. In 1679, New Hampshire became a royal colony. The northern part of the state remained unsettled until 1760, after the French and Indian Wars were over.

New Hampshire took an active part in the American Revolution, although no battles were fought on her soil. The Pine Tree Riot at Weare took place a year prior to the Boston Tea Party, and the capture of Fort William and Mary at New Castle occurred four months before the battles of Lexington and Concord.

On January 5, 1776, a written constitution was adopted by the Provincial Congress at New Hampshire's capital, which at that time was the town of Exeter. This constitution remained in operation until 1784. Thus New Hampshire became the first colony to establish an independent government and declare its independence from Great Britain. General John Stark, hero of Bunker Hill and Bennington, and General John Sullivan, who commanded the capture of Fort William and Mary, were natives of New Hampshire. In 1788, New Hampshire became the ninth state to ratify the federal Constitution.

CHARLESTOWN

OLD FORT NUMBER FOUR: On State Route 11, ½ mile west of the junction of State 11 and 12, and 1 mile east of I-91.

This fort is being reconstructed, using drawings made in 1746 as guides. Several of the buildings are already open—the Great Hall, the watchtower, the stockade, and the houses of Dr. John

Old Fort Number Four

Hastings and Captain Phineas Stevens.

Open: May 15 to October 24, daily from June 5 to Labor Day, weekends only for the rest of the season.

Admission: Nominal fee charged.

CONCORD

A trading post was established here in 1660, but a regular settlement did not exist until the early 1700s because both the Massachusetts and New Hamsphire colonies claimed the lands. It was here that New Hampshire ratified the federal Constitution on June 21, 1788, thus becoming the ninth and deciding state. Concord became the capital of the state in 1808.

DOVER

WILLIAM DAM GARRISON HOUSE: 182-192 Central Avenue.

This house was built by Deacon John Dam (Damme) for his son William about 1675. It was a log cabin surrounded by a stockade and was thus a garrison. According to the Provincial Papers, soldiers were sent to the garrison during the 1690s to assist in guarding against possible attack by the Indians. The house is a perfect example of the fortified home, or garrison, that was so common in New England. There are portholes in the cabin walls through which guns could be fired in case an enemy got inside the stockade.

The building consists of two rooms and has a central chimney. Hand-hewn oak logs, some of them more than 20 feet long, make up the walls. The original windows, which were very small, have been replaced with larger ones. The cabin contains colonial household articles and clothing.

Open: May 30 to November, Tuesday through Sunday, 2 to 5.

Admission: Free.

EXETER

This town, the first capital of New Hampshire, was founded in 1638 by Reverend John Wheelwright.

GARRISON HOUSE: Water and Clifford streets.

The Garrison House, built in 1650, was originally constructed as a blockhouse for protection against the Indians. Later it was converted to an eighteenth-century residence.

CINCINNATI HALL: Water and Governor streets.

Built in 1721, Cincinnati Hall contains furnishings of the Revolutionary era, as well as many personal belongings of the George Washington family.

MANCHESTER

STARK HOUSE: 2000 Elm Street.

General John Stark, the hero of the battles of Bunker Hill and Bennington, lived in this house, which was built by Archibald Stark, the general's father. It is the oldest house in Manchester. A smokeroom and three fireplaces are built around the huge central chimney. The largest of the fireplaces is in the old kitchen, where a beehive oven for baking is built into the side of the chimney. The furnishings are all authentic eighteenth-century pieces typical of those found in the country homes of the time.

Open: May 15 to October 15, Wednesdays and Sundays, 1:30 to 4:30.

Admission: Nominal fee charged.

NEW CASTLE

The narrow streets of this town still retain their early American flavor. Fort William and Mary, a British fortification, was seized by a band of colonial patriots on December 14, 1774, after another ride of warning by Paul Revere. Powder and arms were taken during the raid, stored at Durham, and later used by the patriots at the Battle of Bunker Hill.

FORT POINT LIGHTHOUSE: U.S. Coast Guard Station. The original lighthouse at Fort Point was built in 1771 to replace a lantern hung from a flagstaff at Fort Constitution. The present lighthouse was built in 1877 to replace the first one, which was destroyed by fire in 1869.

PORTSMOUTH

New Hampshire's toehold on the Atlantic Ocean is a 15-mile strip sandwiched between Massachusetts and Maine. It was established by a settlement at the mouth of the Piscataqua River in 1623. The settlers, who had spent two months on the voyage across the Atlantic, feasted on wild strawberries at the river's edge, and thus their new home became known as Strawberry Banke. Twenty years later the town was renamed Portsmouth, in honor of the founder, Captain John Mason, a native of Portsmouth, England.

Portsmouth has many fine examples of colonial architecture in its old houses and narrow, winding streets.

STRAWBERRY BANKE: Old South End. This area is being restored and will, when completed, contain thirty houses, two historic inns, and a statehouse. One building dates from 1660. In the building already open, craftsmen offer demonstrations of such various skills as weaving, spinning, crewel working, and rug, pewter, and cabinet making.

Open: Late May to mid-October, Monday through Saturday 10 to 5, Sunday noon to 5.

Admission: Fee charged; the fee includes a guide. There is a combination ticket that can also be used for Governor Langdon

House, Jackson House, John Paul Jones House, Moffatt-Ladd House, Wentworth-Coolidge Mansion, and the Warner House.

CHASE HOUSE: In Strawberry Banke Restoration.

John Underwood, merchant mariner, built this dwelling in 1762. It was later occupied by Stephen Chase, a Harvard graduate and the son of a minister. Chase became a wealthy Portsmouth merchant with a counting room on Pier Wharf at the foot of State Street. It was Chase who entertained George Washington during the newly elected president's tour of the states in 1789. The house remained in the Chase family until 1881. It is paneled and elaborately carved.

CAPTAIN JOHN CLARK HOUSE: In Strawberry Banke Restoration.

Typical of the area is the design of this house, with its centrally placed entrance doorway, hall, and staircase. The single chimney anchored the structure and heated the rooms. The house was built by William Farrow around 1750 and sold to John Wheelwright soon after it was completed. Then came a series of owners, after which it was purchased, in 1834, by Captain John Clark, Jr., a packetmaster. The house features much paneling and is filled with furnishings of the period.

GOVERNOR JOHN LANGDON MANSION: 143 Pleasant Street.

This is one of the finest Georgian houses in America. It was built in 1784 by John Langdon, Revolutionary leader, one-time governor of New Hampshire, first president of the United States Senate, acting president of the United States prior to the election of George Washington, and the first person to notify Washington of his election to the presidency.

The Langdon mansion has an imposing main stairway, with a balustrade of three different designs to each tread. The newel post is carved from one piece of wood, with its central spiral encased in four spindles of simple design. The mansion's hipped roof is crowned by a captain's walk of Chippendale style.

Open: June through October, Tuesday through Saturday, 10 to 4; closed holidays.

Admission: Nominal fee charged; the combination ticket can be used.

JACKSON HOUSE: Northwest Street.

Richard Jackson, a shipbuilder, constructed this house in 1664. It is a saltbox and is believed to be the oldest frame house in New Hampshire. Its exterior is of weather-stained clapboard.

The house has a large chimney and a sharply sloping gable roof that almost reaches the ground in the rear. There is a lean-to at the rear and one-story frame wings at either end of the main section; these were added in 1764. The original central portion contained a small entrance hall with a parlor to the left and the hall or kitchen to the right.

Open: June through September, Tuesday through Saturday, 1 to 5; closed holidays.

Admission: Nominal fee charged; the combination ticket applies.

JOHN PAUL JONES HOUSE: Middle and State streets.

When John Paul Jones was in Portsmouth to supervise the outfitting of the ship *America,* which was being constructed for the Continental Navy, he lived in this building, then a boarding-house, from October 4 to November 7, 1782. The house was originally built in 1758 by Captain Gregory Purcell, master mariner, who married Sarah Wentworth, niece of Governor Benning Wentworth.

Originally, John Paul Jones came to Portsmouth as commander of the frigate *Ranger,* then under construction. When Jones sailed from Portsmouth on the *Ranger* in November 1777 to carry to the French court news of the great victory at Saratoga, it was the first time that the Stars and Stripes had been raised on the ocean.

Four years later, Jones returned to Portsmouth to supervise the final construction of the *America,* a ship that was eventually given to France by the United States.

Open: May 15 to October 1, weekdays, 10 to 5.

Admission: Nominal fee charged.

MOFFATT-LADD HOUSE: 154 Market Street.

Captain John Moffatt, a wealthy merchant, had ship's carpenters build this house as a wedding gift for his son Samuel in 1763. Captain Moffatt first came into Portsmouth Harbor in 1723 as captain of one of the ships that came to collect masts for the Royal Navy. He remained in Portsmouth to prosper as a shipowner.

When the house was completed, Samuel Moffatt and his bride took possession. But Samuel did not seem to have a head for business and soon found himself heavily in debt. This would have meant imprisonment for him, and so he slipped away to the West Indies. There he made a fresh start, and his family soon followed him.

John Moffatt then moved into the house and lived in it with his daughter and son-in-law, Captain William Whipple, until his death at the age of 94.

William Whipple left the sea and settled in Portsmouth. He was active in the period before the Revolutionary War in provincial affairs and was also active in the Revolution. In 1776 he was sent to the Continental Congress at Philadelphia and was one of the signers of the Declaration of Independence. In 1777, he led New Hampshire troops at the Battle of Saratoga. At the end of the war he ranked as a major-general.

The Whipples were childless, but Mary Tufton Moffatt, daughter of Samuel, married a Dr. Haven. The Havens eventually bought the house for their daughter on her marriage to Alexander Ladd.

The structure stands on high ground overlooking the Piscataqua River. It is a late Georgian, square, three-storied clapboard house with corners accentuated by quoins, three end chimneys, and a hipped roof surmounted by a balustraded captain's walk. The most distinctive features of the house are its handsome flight of granite steps that lead up to the central doorway and the large, paneled entrance hall.

Open: May 15 to October 15, Monday through Saturday 10 to 5; Sunday 2 to 5.

Admission: Nominal fee charged.

ST. JOHN'S CHURCH: Chapel Street.

This church is a successor to Queen's Chapel, which was built in 1732. On November 1, 1789, President George Washington attended services here, and the chair in which he sat now stands within the chancel rail.

In 1717, four copies of the Bible were printed in which the word "vineyard" was misspelled as "vinegar." St. John's Church

has one of these Bibles, known as the "Vinegar Bible."
Open: Monday through Saturday, 8:30 to 3.
Admission: Free.

WARNER HOUSE (MACPHEADRIS-WARNER HOUSE):
Corner of Chapel and Daniels streets.

Captain Archibald Macpheadris, wealthy Scottish fur trader
and iron manager, built this house about 1718 shortly after he
married the daughter of Governor John Wentworth, Sarah
Wentworth. She is said to have received the land as dowry. The
captain had come from Scotland to trade for furs, but later became proprietor of an iron works a few miles inland from
Portsmouth.

Captain Macpheadris' daughter, Mary, married Jonathan
Warner in 1760, and they lived in the house until Warner's
death in 1814. Jonathan Warner had played an important role
in town and provincial affairs. The house remained in the family
until 1931, when it was made a landmark.

The building is thought to be the oldest brick dwelling in
Portsmouth and is one of New England's most significant urban
brick houses still surviving from the early eighteenth century. It
is of early Georgian style, with end chimneys. The two stories
are topped by a dormered gambrel roof and balustrade. The
five-bay main facade has a central doorway capped with broken
sequential arch. The brickwork of the walls is 18 inches thick
and is exposed except on the south end wall, which is clapboarded. The interior has a central hall, with exceptionally fine
frescoes on the walls of the staircase.

Open: Mid-May to mid-October, Monday through Saturday
10 to 5; Sundays 2 to 5.

Admission: Nominal fee charged; the combination ticket
applies.

WENTWORTH-COOLIDGE MANSION: Foot of Little Harbor Road, off U.S. 1A, 2 miles south of Portsmouth.

The earliest part of this rambling frame house dates from
1695. Additions were made in 1750 and in 1830, so that at one
time there were forty rooms, several of which were later removed. The enlarging of the house was done partly to satisfy
the ambitions of the high-living royal governor of the province,

Benning Wentworth, who shocked the community by marrying his pretty, young housekeeper after his wife's death.

Benning Wentworth was appointed the first royal governor of the Province of New Hampshire by King George II in 1741. He died in 1770. Many brilliant social affairs were held in this house and much important business of state was conducted in its council chamber. The mansion was the seat of government when Portsmouth aristocracy was at its height of wealth and fashion.

The west wing was the earliest part of the house and is a typical two-story frame saltbox. In 1730, a two-story frame wing was added to the rear. In 1750, when additional space was needed by the royal governor to carry out his official duties, another two-story wing was added.

On the first floor is the large council chamber with paneled walls and carved mantel which was used for meetings of the governor's council.

Open: Memorial Day to October 12, daily, 10 to 5.

Admission: Nominal fee charged; the combination ticket can be used.

WENTWORTH-GARDNER HOUSE: 140 Mechanic Street.

Ship's carpenters built this house in 1760 for Madame Mark Hunking Wentworth, who presented it to her son Thomas, younger brother of John Wentworth, last royal governor of New Hampshire. It was acquired by Major William Gardner in 1782, and he lived in it until his death in 1833.

The house was built at the water's edge, facing the Piscataqua River. It is two-and-a-half stories high, of wide pine clapboarding that is rusticated to imitate cut stone, with corners emphasized by large quoins. The windows of the first floor are capped by triangular pediments; on the second floor the windows are topped by lintels.

Of standard Georgian design—four rooms with a central hall—the house has a great deal of paneling and carving on the interior. It is said to have taken fourteen months to do the carving.

Many of the fireplaces retain their original Dutch tiles.

The mansion also served as the seat of the state's first colonial government.

Open: May 1 to October 31, Tuesday through Sunday, 1 to 5.

Admission: Nominal fee charged.

Rhode Island

HISTORY

Roger Williams, founder of Rhode Island, was banished from Massachusetts in 1636 for not conforming to the religious ideas practiced there. He purchased some land from the Indians and established the town of Providence, the first permanent settlement in Rhode Island. In 1638, Anne Hutchinson was ousted from Massachusetts and she, her husband, and a small group led by William Coddington and John Clarke founded Pocasset (Portsmouth) on the north end of Aquidneck Island. In 1639, this same group moved south to establish Newport.

Warwick, the fourth settlement, was founded by William Gorton in 1642. The four settlements—Providence, Portsmouth, Newport, and Warwick—united in 1647 and were chartered in 1663 by Charles II as the Colony of Rhode Island and Providence Plantation. In 1664, Block Island joined the colony. The charter of 1663 remained the basis of government of Rhode Island until 1842.

Rhode Island was the first colony to renounce allegiance to Great Britain—on May 4, 1776. The only battle fought on her soil was at Butts Fort in Portsmouth, when the colonists failed in an attempt to drive the British from the island. The British were in control of Newport for three years, thus trapping American ships in Providence. Rhode Island so wanted total independence that only under threat of coercion did she finally ratify the new federal Constitution in 1790—the last state to do so.

ANTHONY

GENERAL NATHANAEL GREENE HOMESTEAD: 20 Taft Street.

Nathanael Greene, who rose rapidly in military rank during the War for Independence and became Washington's second in command, built this fourteen-room house in 1770 while he was in charge of his family's ironworks in Coventry. During the Revolution he exerted such a major influence on the victory in

General Nathanael Greene Homestead

the South, after being sent there to take charge of the operation in October 1780, that the state of Georgia presented him with a plantation for his services. He lived there off and on until his death in 1786.

His house in Anthony has been restored and furnished in the style of the late 1700s.

Open: Wednesdays, Saturdays, and Sundays, 2 to 5, and by appointment; closed December 1 to February 1.

Admission: Free.

BARRINGTON

When this land was purchased from the Indians in 1653, it was divided among Governor William Bradford, Captain Miles Standish, and others of the Pilgrim colony. One of the first settlers was Reverend John Myles, who in 1649 founded the first Baptist Church in the Massachusetts Bay Colony.

BRISTOL

COGGESHELL FARM: Colt State Park.

This is an eighteenth-century Rhode Island farm, which features a restored farm house, blacksmith smithy, barnyard with animals, and a vegetable and herb garden.

Open: July through Labor Day, Saturdays, Sundays, and holidays, 2 to 4.

Admission: Nominal fee charged.

COVENTRY

PAINE HOUSE: 1 Station Street, Washington Village.

Paine House, at one time a colonial inn, was built about 1700. It is now the museum of the Western Rhode Island Civic Historical Society.

Open: May through Labor Day, Tuesdays, 1 to 4; other times by appointment.

Admission: Donation.

EAST GREENWICH

GENERAL JAMES MITCHELL VARNUM HOUSE: 57 Pierce Street.

This colonial mansion is on a hill overlooking Narragansett Bay. It was built for James Mitchell Varnum, who was a lawyer, a Revolutionary general, member of the Continental Congress, director of the Ohio Company, and federal judge for the North-west Territory.

When East Greenwich became aware of the threat of British attack, 54 men formed the Kentish Guards in 1774, with Varnum as their commander. In 1775, he was commissioned a colonel, and he and his brigade took part in the defense of Boston.

In 1777, Varnum was appointed brigadier-general, and, with orders from General Washington, he led his regiments in the battles of Red Bank, Yorktown, Valley Forge, and Rhode Island. His personal friends included Generals Washington, Lafayette, Rochambeau, and Nathanael Greene.

When President Washington tried to open up the Northwest to settlement, he named Varnum, in 1787, to be a United States judge in this territory. The 800-mile journey on horseback to Ohio proved to be too much for Varnum, and seven months after his arrival in Marietta, Ohio, he died at the age of 40.

The Varnum mansion has double chimneys and eight fireplaces. On the second floor is the chamber used by Lafayette on his visits to East Greenwich.

Open: Sundays, June through September, also Wednesdays, July through September, 3 to 5; by appointment all year round.

Admission: Donation.

JOHNSTON

CLEMENCE IRONS HOUSE: 38 George Waterman Road (4 miles northwest of Providence).

One of the oldest houses in Rhode Island, it was built in 1679.

Open: May to mid-October, upon application at caretaker's house.

Admission: Nominal fee charged.

LINCOLN WOODS RESERVATION STATE PARK

ELEAZER ARNOLD HOUSE: 448 Great Road.

"Stone-ender" houses were popular in Rhode Island because of the locality's abundant supply of building stone and lime for mortar. This house, erected in 1687, is a fine example of the style. When first built, it had only one room, with a fireplace at one end. Later a kitchen was added in a rear lean-to, and a new chamber was built and joined to the original one. The chimney became so wide it almost covered the end of the house.

In the eighteenth century the house was enlarged again—the roof was raised over the rear to form two full stories. A two-room deep, two-story frame section with a separate chimney was added at the east, and another one-story lean-to was built across the rear. The original high-peaked front gable was removed at the time.

The house has an imposing chimney top and a huge hall fireplace with an oak mantel more than 12 feet long.

Open: June 15 to October 15, daily except Mondays. At other times, apply to the custodian in an adjacent house.
Admission: Donations.

MIDDLETOWN

WHITEHALL: 20 miles southeast, on Berkeley Avenue at the head of Paradise Avenue.

Dean George Berkeley, Irish philosopher, built this home in 1729. The furnishings date from the late seventeenth and early eighteenth centuries.

Open: July 1 through Labor Day, daily, 1 to 5.

Admission: Nominal fee charged; also by strip ticket sold by the Preservation Society of Newport County, 37 Touro Street, Newport.

NEWPORT

The city of Newport, settled in 1639, was building ships as early as 1646. It was a prosperous port, rivaling both Boston and New York, and the town still has the appearance of a colonial seaport. Many of Newport's ships were slave traders and privateers.

NEWPORT HISTORIC DISTRICT: Bounded by Van Zandt Avenue, Farewell, Sherman, High, Thomas, Golden Hill, Thames, Marsh, and Washington streets.

There are many Georgian structures in this area that illustrate mid-eighteenth-century architectural history. Because of the work of Richard Munday, master carpenter, and Peter Harrison, a distinguished colonial architect, Newport's Georgian public buildings are considered to be among the finest built in the colonies during the eighteenth century. But there are also rows of small eighteenth-century dwellings and shops that still occupy the old part of the city. The historic structures are largely concentrated near the waterfront, within the eighteenth-century limits of the town.

NEWPORT HISTORICAL SOCIETY: 82 Touro Street.

Three connected buildings of the society include the Seventh Day Baptist Church, which was built in 1729. The other two house a marine museum and displays of costumes, furnishings, and Indian relics.

Open: Tuesdays through Fridays, 9:30 to 4:30; Saturdays, 9:30 to noon. Closed Sundays, Mondays, and during December.

Admission: Free.

BRICK MARKET: Thomas Street and Washington Square.

The Brick Market, built in 1762, was originally constructed with open facades on the ground level for the produce market; the two upper floors were devoted to retail drygoods and offices. The building was later used as a theater, from 1793 to 1799. It served as town and city hall from 1842 to 1900, and now it holds the offices of the Newport Chamber of Commerce.

Open: Mondays through Saturdays, 10 to 5.

Admission: Free.

FRIENDS MEETINGHOUSE: 30 Marlborough Street.

This is one of the first meetinghouses on American soil. The oldest part of the building dates from 1699.

HUNTER HOUSE (NICHOLS-WANTON-HUNTER HOUSE): 54 Washington Street.

In 1719, James Sheffield was given a tract of land where this house stands. He sold the land to Deputy Jonathan Nichols in 1748. It is not known whether Sheffield or Nichols—or neither—built the house that is there today. Nichols was a successful merchant, proprietor of the White Horse Tavern and owner of at least one privateer.

The house has brick-filled walls, plastered over in the English half-timbered tradition. It is one of the most luxurious in Newport. The pineapple carving—symbol of hospitality—is one of the few decorations on the dignified exterior.

After Nichols died in 1754, Joseph Wanton, Jr., became the owner. Wanton, Jr., served as lieutenant governor in 1764 and 1767. His father was governor from 1768 through 1775, when he was deposed. The Wantons were Loyalists in sentiment, and they fled to the British in New York during the Revolution. The house in Newport was confiscated and became the quarters of the ailing Admiral deTernay, commander of the French fleet that arrived in Newport in 1780. It was in one of the upstairs parlors, which he had used as a bedroom, that deTernay died. He was buried in nearby historic Trinity churchyard.

The house is an early New England Georgian two-story building with a balustraded gambrel roof. It has two exterior chimneys and the typical Georgian floor plan of two rooms on either side of the central hall on both floors. It contains fine paneling, furniture, paintings, and silver.

Open: June 1 through October 1, daily, 10 to 5; during the rest of the year by appointment.

Admission: Adults, nominal fee charged; children under 6, free.

Hunter Museum

MEMORIAL PARK: Bounded by Admiral Kalbfuss Road, Girard Avenue, and Hillside Avenue.

The park was originally part of the land purchased in 1637 from the Narragansett Indians. The colonists used the hill as a lookout, for public executions, and for beacons. In 1776, Colonel Israel Putnam constructed fortifications here, which were strengthened by the British when they captured Newport. The remains of the British powder magazine and other works are still visible.

Open: Daily.

Admission: Nominal fee charged.

OLD COLONY HOUSE (OLD STATE HOUSE): Washington Square.

The building was erected in 1739. It housed the General Assembly of the colony of Rhode Island and, from 1790 to 1900, the Rhode Island legislature. The Declaration of Independence was read from its balcony. When General Washington came to Newport to visit the newly arrived French Army during the Revolutionary War, a banquet was held in the great hall. The federal Constitution was ratified here in 1790. And for 150 years the building was the scene of gubernatorial inaugurations.

Old Colony House is a red brick building with a gable roof surmounted by a two-story octagonal cupola. The dominant feature of the main facade is the center doorway and balcony.

Open: May 31 to September 1, daily, 9:30 to noon and 1 to 4; closed Saturdays and Sundays during the rest of the year.

Admission: Free.

REDWOOD LIBRARY: 50 Bellevue Avenue.

The Redwood Library was the outgrowth of a philosophical society founded in Newport in 1730. In 1747, Abraham Redwood donated funds for the purchase of books, which became the nucleus of the library. The building, one of the oldest libraries in continuous use in the United States, contains many valuable books and early American paintings, including six by Gilbert Stuart.

Open: Weekdays, 10 to 6.

Admission: Free.

TOURO SYNAGOGUE: 72 Touro Street.

In 1647, Roger Williams proclaimed religious liberty in the Rhode Island colony. Ten years later a Jewish colony settled in Newport. Their synagogue, today known as the Touro Synagogue, was dedicated in 1763 by Rabbi Isaac Touro.

The building was originally designed in the Georgian style, but was modified to accommodate the Sephardic ritual. The synagogue is the oldest one in America. Congregation Jeshuel Israel—Salvation of Israel—still worships there.

The interior of the building is considered to be an architectural masterpiece. Twelve Ionic columns support the gallery, above which rise Corinthian columns supporting a domed ceiling. The holy Ark at the east end contains sacred, hand-lettered Scrolls of the Law, mounted on wooden rollers.

Open: From the last week in June to Labor Day, Mondays through Fridays 10 to 5, Sundays 10 to 6; closed Saturdays except for services at 9 A.M.: during the rest of the year, Sundays from 2 to 4. Services are held Fridays at 7:30 P.M.

Admission: Free.

TRINITY CHURCH: 141 Spring Street.

This early New England Georgian frame church was built in 1726 and is closely modeled after Boston's Old North (Christ) Church. It is rectangular, with arched windows on two levels and a projecting front tower and spire, which is still tipped with the golden crown of England. The building was made larger in 1762. Episcopal services are still being held in the church today.

Open: June 15 to Labor Day, daily, 10 to 5; during the rest of the year by appointment.

Admission: Free.

WANTON-LYMAN-HAZARD HOUSE: 82 Touro Street.

This is the oldest house in Newport, probably built about 1695. It illustrates the architectural transition from the seventeenth to the eighteenth century. Its frame construction is reminiscent of the houses of early New England, while all the structural detail and ornamentation reflect the changes that developed into the Georgian style of middle colonial times.

The first mention of the house dates from 1724, when Richard Ward, later governor of the Rhode Island colony, bought it from Stephen Mumford. The house was damaged by the Stamp Act riots in 1765, when it was occupied by Martin Howard, the Tory stamp master.

The house originally was a two-and-a-half-story structure with rooms on both sides of the central chimney and a kitchen ell at the rear. The chimney is of brick rather than stone, although brick was not common in Rhode Island prior to the eighteenth century. In later years a lean-to was built across the back, dormer and sash windows were installed, and a classic doorway was added. Most of the furnishings are of the 1700s with a few earlier pieces.

Open: July 1 to Labor Day, daily, 10 to 5.

Admission: Nominal fee charged.

PAWTUCKET

DAGGETT HOUSE: Slater Park, off U.S. 1A.

The present Daggett House, built in 1685 and remodeled in 1790, replaced one built in 1644 by John Daggett. The earlier one burned down during the King Philip's War.

The Daggetts were slaveholders, and in one of the beams of the house can be seen a ring from which a slave's hammock had been hung. In the attic is a secret closet where the family could hide from Indians. The house is filled with furnishings owned by Samuel Slater and General and Mrs. Nathanael Greene.

Open: June to mid-September, Sundays, 2 to 5; during the rest of the year, by appointment with the Pawtucket Chapter of the DAR.

PORTSMOUTH

At one time, Portsmouth, founded in 1638, was the most populated town in the colony. The first settlers landed at Founders' Brook on Boyd's Lane. A bronze tablet on Pudding Rock is inscribed with a copy of the Portsmouth Compact.

FRIEND'S MEETINGHOUSE: Middle Road and Hedley Street.

During the Revolution this meetinghouse, which had been in use since 1700, was occupied by American troops. A Quaker school was founded here in November, 1784, but in 1819 the school was moved to Providence.

PROVIDENCE

Roger Williams named this city in gratitude "for God's merciful providence unto me in my diestree." In its early days it was a shipping and shipbuilding town, running the Triangular Trade route with slaves, rum, and molasses between Africa, the West Indies, and the colonies.

CATHEDRAL OF ST. JOHN: 271 North Main Street.
In the early days the cathedral was known as King's Church. Founded in 1722, it is the oldest Episcopal church in the city and one of the four colonial parishes in the state. The communion silver was given by Queen Anne.
Open: Daily, 8 to 4:30.
Admission: Free.

JOHN BROWN HOUSE: 52 Power Street.
John Quincy Adams said of this house it was "the most magnificent and elegant mansion that I have ever seen on this continent." The house is a fine example of Georgian architecture and was built in 1786 by John Brown, a wealthy Quaker merchant and brother of architect Joseph Brown. It has three stories, four exterior chimneys, massive brick walls, and interior brick partitions. There is a central, pedimented pavilion and a balustraded Doric portico. Inside, there is the usual Georgian plan of two rooms on each side of a central hall on each floor, and much beautifully carved woodwork. The large brick service wing at the rear of the house was added at a later date. The house contains furnishings and china related to the period.
Open: Tuesday through Friday, 11 to 4, Saturdays and Sundays, 2 to 4; closed Mondays and holidays.
Admission: Nominal fee charged.

FIRST BAPTIST MEETINGHOUSE: North Main Street between Waterman and Thomas streets.
The meetinghouse is one of New England's most notable colonial public buildings, both in its architecture and history. It was built in 1774 by Joseph Brown, amateur architect, from designs based on plans of English churches, and it was dedicated in May, 1775, a few weeks after the outbreak of the Revolution. It was built "for the worship of God and to hold college commencements in." Since that time Brown University has held its commencements there.

The church was originally 80 feet square, with a door on each side and the main entrance under the spire on the west end; there are two tiers of round-headed windows on each side. The tower and spire rise 185 feet above the ground. Originally, it had a slave gallery, which was removed in later remodelings of the church.

Open: May through October, Monday through Saturday, 9 to 4; November through April, Monday through Saturday, 11 to 2; closed holidays. Tours are conducted following Sun-

Exterior, First Baptist Church

Interior, First Baptist Church

day services.
Admission: Free.

BETSY WILLIAMS COLLEGE HOUSE: Roger Williams Park, near the Elmwood Avenue entrance.

A descendant of Roger Williams, who gave the first 100 acres of land to establish the park named in his honor, once owned this house. It contains colonial furniture and items of historic interest dating from 1773, when the house was built.

Open: Check locally.
Admission: Check locally.

UNIVERSITY HALL: Brown University campus.

Brown University was chartered at Warren, Rhode Island, in 1764 as Rhode Island College, but was relocated in Providence in 1770, at which time University Hall was built. During the American Revolution it was used as a barracks and hospital.

For tours, apply to the Admissions Office, Brown University.
Admission: Free.

STEPHEN HOPKINS HOUSE: Benefit and Hopkins streets. This house was built about 1707 and added to in 1743. It became the home of Stephen Hopkins, who was governor of Rhode Island ten times, a member of the Continental Congress, a signer of the Declaration of Independence, and the first chancellor of Brown University. Of his signing of the Declaration of Independence Hopkins said, "My hand trembled but my heart does not."

Open: Wednesdays and Saturdays, 1 to 4, year round.
Admission: Free.

TIVERTON

CHASE-CORY HOUSE: Main Road, Tiverton Four Corners. Built about 1730, this house is furnished in the style of the period.

Open: May through October, Sundays, 2 to 4:30; July and August, Sundays and Wednesdays, 2 to 4:30.
Admission: Free.

FORT BARTON: Highland Road.
Fort Barton was built during the American Revolution as an area for the massing of troops. It was used for the invasion of Aquidneck Island and Newport and the eventual Battle of Rhode Island.

Open: Daily.
Admission: Free.

WICKFORD

OLD NARRAGANSETT CHURCH: Main Street.
The original church was erected in 1707 on Gongdon Hill. It is the oldest Episcopal church building north of Virginia and is one of the four original colonial parishes in the state. The church has a wine-glass pulpit and a slave gallery. The silver communion service, still in use, was presented to the church in 1710 by Queen Anne.

Open: July and August, Fridays, 2 to 4; Sunday services in August at 9:30 and 6; the church can be seen at other times by appointment.

Admission: Donations.

SMITH'S CASTLE: 1½ miles north of U.S. 1

It is believed that Smith's Castle is the only house still stand-ing in which Roger Williams once lived, wrote, and preached to the Indians. Richard Smith built it in 1637 as a substantial forti-fied dwelling in the midst of "the thickest of the barbarians." It was burned in 1676 and rebuilt in 1678, again by Richard Smith. The interior was remodeled in 1740.

The eighteenth-century garden is worth a visit.

Open: Weekdays, except Thursdays, 10 to 5; Sundays, 2 to 5; closed December 15 to March 15.

Admission: Nominal fee charged.

Massachusetts

HISTORY

The history of Massachusetts begins with the exploration of its coast by John Cabot, the Italian explorer, in 1497-98. Bartholomew Gosnold, an English navigator, discovered and named Cape Cod in 1602.

When the Pilgrims landed at Cape Cod in the early winter of 1620, they found that they were so far north they were out of the jurisdiction of the Virginia Company, which had granted them a patent. Finding themselves without warrant, in bad weather, and with many dissenting members, they drew up the Mayflower Compact to serve as a foundation for their government. They then sailed across Cape Cod Bay and landed at Plymouth on December 21, 1620. This was the first permanent settlement in Massachusetts. A colony had been started in 1602 on Cuttyhunk Island, but it lasted only a few days.

The settling of Plymouth was followed by the establishment of Salem, Charlestown, and Boston. By 1640, there were about 2,500 people living in eight settlements.

The Puritan exodus from Europe was as much for economic reasons as for religious beliefs, but the religious freedom they did seek for themselves was not granted by them to others. The result was that those who disagreed with their beliefs—the Quakers, the Baptists, the Jews—were banished from Massachusetts and went south to settle Rhode Island and Connecticut.

In 1692, the Massachusetts Bay and Plymouth colonies were united under a royal governor, Sir Williams Phipps. When England in later years took stringent measures to control the colony, it paved the way for the Boston Tea Party, the closing of Boston Harbor, and the organization of the Minutemen.

The American Revolution began in Massachusetts, at Lexington and Concord. And in 1788, Massachusetts became the sixth state to ratify the Constitution.

AMESBURY

ROCKY HILL MEETINGHOUSE

The original meetinghouse was constructed in 1716. Many years later, when the building needed repair, it was decided to erect a new meetinghouse at a new location. The new structure was the Rocky Hill Meetinghouse, built in 1785.

In this meetinghouse, Abigail Eastman was married to Ebenizer Webster, a widower from Salisbury, New Hampshire. Daniel Webster was one of their three children.

The building is a very simple one and looks like a house from the exterior—a house with three doors. There is no belfry or steeple. The pulpit is elaborately carved, and the pews are of handsome, aged pine. There is a gallery on three sides, where the young men and women sat facing each other.

Open: May through October, weekdays, 9 to 5.

Admission: Voluntary contributions.

ARLINGTON

JASON RUSSELL HOUSE: 7 Jason Street.

Jason Russell was 58 years old and lame on the opening day of the War for Independence, April 19, 1775. He led his family to safety and then returned to defend his home. A group of Minutemen took refuge in his house, and Russell and eleven of the Minutemen were killed by the pursuing British.

The gray clapboard house was erected prior to 1680. Two rooms were furnished in seventeenth- and eighteenth-century style.

Open: April to November, Tuesday through Saturday, 2 to 5; at other times by appointment.

Admission: Voluntary contribution.

BEVERLY

BALCH HOUSE: 448 Cabot Street.

This house stands on part of a land grant given the "Old Painters" in 1635. It was built in 1636 and was occupied by the Balch family until 1914. It is one of the oldest frame houses in the country.

Open: June 15 through September 15, Monday through Saturday, 9 to 4; closed holidays; open at other times by appointment.
Admission: Nominal fee charged.

JOHN CABOT HOUSE: 117 Cabot Street.

The John Cabot House, now used by the Beverly Historical Society, was built in 1781. Period furnishings, paintings, ships' logs, and other early relics are on display.
Open: July and August, Monday through Saturday, 10 to 4; September through June, Mondays, Wednesdays, Fridays, and Saturdays, 10 to 4; closed on holidays.
Admission: Nominal fee charged.

JOHN JALE HOUSE: 39 Hale Street.

John Jale was the first minister of Beverly, and he built this house in 1694.
Open: June 15 to September 15, Tuesday through Saturday, 10 to 4.
Admission: Voluntary contribution.

BOSTON

Boston was settled by a company of men under the leadership of John Winthrop in 1630. In 1632, Boston became the capital of the Massachusetts Bay Colony, and as the years went on the city continued to expand.

In 1770, the "Boston Massacre" took place near the old State House, when British troops fired on a mob of citizens, killing six. In 1773, the Boston Tea Party was held and the port was closed by the British Parliament.

On April 19, 1775, the British attempted to seize the military stores of the colonial militia at Concord. It was then that Paul Revere made his famous ride, calling Minutemen to arms. The American Revolution started that day at Lexington, and the Battle of Bunker Hill resulted. In 1776, George Washington, as commander-in-chief of the Continental Army, mounted cannon on Dorchester Heights and drove the British out of Boston.

There are so many things to see in Boston that it might be best to visit the information center on the Boylston Street side of the Boston Common and obtain self-guided tour maps, brochures, and current events information. The center is open daily until 5.

KING'S CHAPEL: Tremont and School streets.

The original church was built on this site in 1687; but Peter Harrison designed a new church and it was constructed in the years 1749-54. The new church was built around the old wooden structure. The congregation continued to worship while the new building was being erected. When the new structure was completed, the old one was torn down and thrown out the windows.

King's Chapel was built to serve the officers of the British Crown. It was the first Anglican church in Puritan Boston—and highly unpopular. Because of anti-royalist sentiment, it was known as "Stone Chapel" for many years after the American Revolution.

The church is an excellent example of Georgian church architecture in the American colonies. The main portion of the rectangle is built of cut Quincy granite; the square stone base for the tower was intended to carry a spire, but this was never added. The original plans included a front porch with stone Ionic columns 25 feet high, but these were not built until 1785-87—and then of wood.

The Governor's Pew was used originally by the royal governors and later by important colonial personages. President Washington sat in it on October 27, 1789, at a concert given to raise money for the present portico. King's Chapel burying ground contains the graves of Governor John Winthrop, Reverend John Cotton, John Davenport, founder of New Haven, and Lady Andros.

Open: Daily, 10 to 4; Sunday services at 11.
Admission: Free.

OLD NORTH CHURCH (CHRIST CHURCH): 193 Salem Street.

The Old North Church was built in 1723 by William Price, a book and print seller of Boston, from designs based on Christopher Wren's great London churches. When a 1954 hurricane blew over the steeple, the window from which Paul Revere's lanterns gleamed was saved and put back into the steeple along with the other ancient woodwork. Revere's lanterns were hung in the belfry on the night of April 18, 1775, to alert patriots on the other side of the Charles River that British troops were moving out of Boston by water ("one if by land, two if by sea").

Old North Church is the oldest surviving church in Boston. It contains a restored organ, constructed in 1759, and one of the earliest banks of bells on this continent.

Open: Daily, 9 to 4; Sunday services at 11.
Admission: Free.

THE COMMON

Boston Common is the oldest public park in the country. The land was set aside in 1634 for common use as a "cow pasture and training field." The stock and pens that the Puritans used to punish religious offenders were placed on the Common, and here the British mustered before the Battle of Bunker Hill.

FANEUIL HALL: Dock Square.

It was in this hall that James Otis, Samuel Adams, and other leaders of the opposition to the Crown built colonial dissent into powerful sentiment for American self-government. For this reason the building is often called "the Cradle of Liberty."

Peter Faneuil, an outstanding merchant of Boston, offered the market house to the city in 1740. This offer was accepted by a narrow margin, since the countrymen favored door-to-door peddling while the city dwellers preferred a central market. On September 10, 1742, Faneuil Hall was completed. It had been designed in Georgian style, two stories high, with open arcades for the public market on the ground floor. The long room above the marketplace was designed to serve for town meetings and municipal affairs.

The hall was destroyed by fire on January 13, 1761, but it was rebuilt in 1763. By 1768, the hall had become too small for the town meetings, which were often moved to the Old South Meeting House.

During the siege of Boston by the British, the hall was used as a playhouse for amateur theatricals offered by the British officers and Tory ladies in town.

After the Revolution, the building was enlarged several times. It now contains historical paintings of famous battles as well as a military museum and library.

Open: Monday through Friday, 9 to 5; Saturdays, 9 to noon; Sundays, 1 to 5. Library, armory, and museum are open Monday through Friday, 10 to 4.

Admission: Free.

HARRISON GARY OTIS HOUSE: 141 Cambridge Street. Now headquarters of the Society for the Preservation of New England antiquities, the Harrison Gary Otis house was built in 1796. The New England Museum of Antiquities is connected to this house.

Open: Monday through Friday, 10 to 4; closed holidays.

Admission: Nominal fee charged.

OLD SOUTH MEETING HOUSE: Washington and Milk streets.

This church was built in 1729 to replace the Cedar Meetinghouse built in 1669 by dissenters from the First Congregational Church of Boston. The building was the scene of many protest meetings prior to the American Revolution, because of its large seating capacity. In many instances even this building could not accommodate all the people who gathered to protest against England.

The famous meeting that started the Boston Tea Party was held here on December 16, 1773; over 4,000 people attended. It was here in 1775 that a riding school for British troops was established by order of General Burgoyne. Pews and pulpits were torn away and broken up. When General Washington made his triumphal entry into Boston in March of 1776, he paused, entered the building, and looked down from the eastern gallery on the scene of desolation.

This is among the few pre-Revolutionary meetinghouses still standing. It was originally erected in 1669; the present building dates from 1729. It now contains collections of relics.

Open: June 1 to September, Monday through Friday, 9 to 5, Saturdays, 10 to 5; October 1 through May, Monday through Saturday, 9 to 4; closed Thanksgiving, Christmas, and New Year's Day.

Admission: Adults, nominal fee charged; children under 12, free.

OLD STATE HOUSE: Washington and State streets.

This structure is often called the "second Boston Town House" as it was erected in 1713 on the site of the first town house, which had been built in 1658. It was the seat of government of provincial Massachusetts, the meeting place for colonial courts, and the scene of many civic and military affairs.

In February, 1761, James Otis helped to ignite the Revolutionary movements with his impassioned speech in the Old State House against the legality of the Writs of Assistance (search warrants) which made possible the search of all premises for possible smuggled goods.

It was at the east front of the building that the Boston Massacre took place; from the balcony facing State Street the Declaration of Independence was proclaimed. George Washington was on another balcony of the State House when he reviewed the honor parade in 1789.

The building served as the state house of the Commonwealth of Massachusetts from 1776 to 1798. John Hancock was inaugurated as the first governor of Massachusetts here in 1780.

Today the building houses the Bostonian Society and its collection of relics, including tea from the Boston Tea Party. There also is an exhibit on Boston shipping and a display of works by Paul Revere, who was also a renowned silversmith.

Open: Monday through Saturday, 9 to 4; closed January 1, Thanksgiving, and Christmas.

Admission: Free.

GRANARY BURYING GROUND: Tremont Street at the head of Bromfield Street.

Among the patriots buried at Granary are John Hancock, Samuel Adams, Robert Treat Paine, Paul Revere, Peter Faneuil, the parents of Benjamin Franklin, and the victims of the Boston Massacre.

Open: Daily, 8 to 4.
Admission: Free.

BOSTON LIGHT: Little Brewster Island, Boston Harbor.
Little Brewster Island is the site of the first lighthouse in
North America. The first lighthouse was built in 1716 and
destroyed by the British in 1776. Known as the Boston Light,
it was reconstructed in 1783 according to the plan of the old
lighthouse, probably incorporating the remaining wall of the
island's old town. The 89-foot tower is a combination of rub-
ble stone, granite, and brick. It is now operated by the United
States Coast Guard.

PAUL REVERE HOUSE: 19-21 North Square.
The home of Paul Revere is the only extant seventeenth-century dwelling in downtown Boston. It was occupied by Paul
Revere for about five years before the outbreak of the Revolution, and it was from this house that he left for his famous ride
on the night of April 18, 1775.
It is believed that when the house was originally built about
1676, it was a one-room house, two-and-a-half-stories high,
with an end chimney, but when Revere moved into it almost
one hundred years later, he enlarged it to a full three stories.
The original house was probably built by John Jeffs on the site
of the Increase Mather parsonage shortly after the great Boston
fire of 1676.
During the nineteenth century, the building became a tene-
ment and was used as a store, but in 1908 it was restored by
architect Joseph Everitt Chandler and furnished in the eighteenth-century style.
Open: Monday through Saturday, 9 to 3:45; closed Sundays
and holidays.
Admission: Adults, nominal fee charged; children under 14,
free.

PIERCE-HICHBORN HOUSE: 29 North Square.
The house is typical of many of the seventeenth-century,
pre-Georgian brick dwellings erected in Boston to replace
earlier wooden buildings destroyed in the great fire of 1676.
Moses Pierce, an artisan-glazier, built the three-story, hipped-
roof dwelling for his family. It is a six-room house, constructed
of red brick laid in English bond. An addition to the house was

made in the eighteenth century.

In 1781, Nathaniel Hichborn acquired the dwelling, and his family owned it until 1864. It is now a history museum.

Open: May 1 to October 31, daily except Mondays, 10 to 6; November 1 to April 30, weekdays 10 to 5, Sundays 2 to 3; closed Tuesdays and holidays.

Admission: Nominal fee charged.

CAMBRIDGE

CHRIST CHURCH: Garden Street, opposite George Washington Memorial Gateway.

Christ Church was built between 1759 and 1761, on a design by the great Peter Harrison. It was the religious center for Cambridge aristocrats until the outbreak of the Revolution. The Common in front of the church was a mustering ground for American troops.

In December, 1775, Martha Washington requested that the church be readied for religious services. On New Year's Eve, and occasionally afterward, services were held there during Washington's stay in Cambridge. By the time the British evacuated Boston in March of 1776, most of the Loyalist Anglican congregation had left, and the church was used as a barracks by the Americans. After Burgoyne's surrender at Saratoga in October, 1777, his captive army was held for a time in Cambridge. When a funeral service was held in the church for a young British officer, a mob attacked the building and damaged it. Services in the building were not resumed until 1970.

The entrance of this Georgian church is formed by a low wood tower, which is topped by a smaller cruciform belfry. There is planking on each side, broken by a row of seven arched windows. The building is designed as a typical Anglican church, with nave, side aisles, and a focus on the altar. Six free-standing raised class columns along each side of the nave support the ceiling over the aisles. Two bays were added to the nave in 1857.

Vassall-Craigie-Longfellow House

VASSALL-CRAIGIE-LONGFELLOW HOUSE: 105 Battle Street.

Known also as the John Vassall House or the Longfellow House, this fine building has had quite a history, from the time it was built in 1759 by John Vassall until the death of Henry Wadsworth Longfellow in 1882.

When the handsome old mansion was built, it was surrounded by a park of 150 acres. The Vassall family was Loyalist, which seems surprising when one reads their background. The first John Vassall of whom there is mention was an alderman in London, England. In 1588, he fitted out two ships and joined the Royal Navy in the expedition against the Spanish Armada. His sons, Samuel and William, were both original patentees of lands in the Massachusetts colony; although Samuel never came to this country, he has a monument in King's Chapel, Boston, that proclaims him as "the first who boldly refused to submit to the tax tonnage and poundage imposed by the Crown." He was imprisoned and his goods seized because of this protest. Later on, Cromwell's Parliament voted him more than 10,000 pounds damages.

Samuel seems to have received little of this sum, for in 1657, he (or his heirs) claimed that more than 3,000 pounds were due for "services of one ship," and another *(Mayflower)* had "when laden and manned, been taken and made use of against the enemy." One would not expect this man to be on the side of the Crown; had he come to the colonies, he probably would not have been.

His brother, William, was the first Vassall to come to America. With his wife and six children, he set sail in 1635. He settled first at Roxbury and later removed to Scituate. In 1646, William returned to England to pursue a petition for redress of wrongs. He never returned to Massachusetts, but went to Barbados, where he died.

William's son John lived in Jamaica, but John's son Major Leonard Vassal, born on that island in 1678, went to Boston before 1723 with his wife and some of his sixteen children. When his wife died, Leonard married again and had another daughter.

From July, 1775, to April, 1776, the house was used by General Washington as headquarters. War conferences were held within its walls. It is said that the room on the second floor, later used by Longfellow as his study, was the scene of these meetings.

The house is a big square building, with a classic portico, pillars supporting a pediment, topped by a fanlight. There is paneling of oak and carved oaken chimney-pieces. The walls are hung with tapestries and further adorned with artistic cabinets and clocks.

Open: May through October, Monday through Friday, 10 to 5; Saturdays, noon to 5; Sundays, 1 to 5. The remainder of the year, Monday through Friday, 10 to 4; Saturdays and Sundays, 2 to 4.

Admission: Nominal fee charged.

MASSACHUSETTS HALL: Harvard University Yard.

Massachusetts Hall is the oldest surviving building of the first colonial institution for higher learning. It was designed by Harvard presidents John Leverett and his successor, Benjamin Wadsworth, and was built during the years 1718-20. It was originally a dormitory containing a chamber and a small private study for each of the 64 students. During the siege of Boston, 640 American soldiers took quarters in the hall. Much of the interior woodwork and hardware, including brass doorknobs, disappeared at that time.

It now houses the administrative offices for Harvard University.

Open: Check locally.

COOPER-FROST-AUSTIN HOUSE: 21 Linnaean Street.

When it was originally built in 1657, this house stood on a grassy way that was called "Lovelane"; the Common, where the citizens pastured their cows, extended from Harvard Square up to its front door. Behind the building there was a garden that sloped upward to Gallows Hill.

It is the oldest house in Cambridge and is in excellent condition.

After the death of Walter Cooper III, his widow married Jonathan Hill. Two children were born of that marriage, Jonathan Cooper Hill in 1763 and Lydia in 1766. When Lydia was baptized in the meetinghouse in the college yard, there was present a student named Jeremiah Fogg of Kensington, New Hampshire, who vowed that he would one day marry the little Lydia. When Lydia was 19 years of age, the American Revolution broke out, and Major Jeremiah Fogg came to Cambridge with his New Hampshire men. He renewed his acquaintance with Lydia, and some years later he did marry her. Outside the west parlor of the house the red lilac that Lydia planted in 1775 still blooms in the spring.

The original thick oak beams and most of the old wooden clapboard, fastened with hand-wrought nails, are still intact. The ceilings are low. Around the central chimney are grouped several large fireplaces, each with a huge beam across the top.

Open: June through October, Mondays and Thursdays 2 to 5, Tuesdays 7 to 9; November 10 to May, Thursdays 2 to 5, Tuesdays 7 to 9.

Admission: Nominal fee charged.

CAPE COD AREA

BARNSTABLE

CROCKER TAVERN: ¼ mile west on State 6A.
During the eighteenth century there was a stagecoach route between Barnstable and Boston; the Crocker Tavern, built in 1745, was a scheduled stop on this route. The tavern is now furnished in eighteenth-century antiques.
Open: Mid-June to mid-October, Tuesdays, Thursdays, and Saturdays, 1 to 5.
Admission: Adults, nominal fee charged; children under 14, free.

BREWSTER

OLD GRISTMILL: 2 miles west off State 6A on Stony Brook Road.
During the summer months, corn is still ground at the old Gristmill. It stands on the site of one of the oldest gristmills in the country.
Open: Wednesdays, Fridays, and Saturdays, 2 to 5.
Admission: Free.

CHATHAM

ATWOOD HOUSE: 1 mile south of Chatham.
The oldest house in Chatham, Atwood House is filled with antique furnishings.
Open: Late June through mid-September, Mondays, Wednesdays, and Fridays, 2 to 5.
Admission: Nominal fee charged.

EASTHAM

The Pilgrims' first encounter with Indians took place here in December, 1620.

OLD WINDMILL: Near the town hall.
Corn is still occasionally ground here in the oldest windmill on Cape Cod. It was built in 1693.

Open: Last week in June to September 14, Monday through Saturday 10 to noon and 1 to 5, Sundays 1 to 5.
Admission: Free.

SANDWICH

DEXTER'S GRISTMILL: Main Street.
Corn is ground daily at this mill, which was built in 1654.
Open: June 15 to October 1, daily, 10 to 5.
Admission: Nominal fee charged; combination ticket to the Gristmill and Hoxie House can be used.

HOXIE HOUSE: ¼ mile east on State 130.
Abraham Hoxie, a whaling captain for whom the house is named, bought this saltbox in 1858. It dates from 1637. The furnishings are from the 1680-90 period.
Open: June 15 to October 1, daily, 10 to 5.
Admission: Adults, nominal fee charged; children under 12, free.

WEST BARNSTABLE

WEST PARISH MEETINGHOUSE (Congregational): 1 mile south on State 149, at the junction with U.S. 6.
One of the oldest Congregational church buildings in the country, the West Parish Meetinghouse was built in 1717 as an offshoot of the First Congregational Church in London. A Paul Revere bell, cast in 1806, and a steeple clock brought from England in 1723 are the highlights of the building.
Open: Daily, 9 to 5.
Admission: Free.

CONCORD

It was here in Concord that John Hancock presided over the First Provincial Congress and that the Minutemen were organized. The town was settled in 1635.
On April 19, 1775, 800 British troops who had marched from Boston to seize the war supplies stored in Concord were met by the Minutemen. By the "rude bridge that arches the floor," the Battle of Concord was fought.

The Old Manse

OLD MANSE: Monument Street.

Reverend William Emerson, grandfather of Ralph Waldo Emerson, constructed the manse in 1765. The Emerson family watched the battle at the North Bridge in 1775 from a second-story window.

Open: June 1 to October 15, Tuesday through Saturday 10 to 4:40, Sundays 1 to 4:30; April 19 to Memorial Day, and October 15 to November 11, Saturdays 10 to 4:30, Sundays and holidays 1 to 4:30.

Admission: Nominal fee charged.

MINUTEMAN NATIONAL HISTORICAL PARK

When completed, this park will encompass the areas between Concord and Lexington. Visitors may obtain information from the office in the Buttrick Mansion, overlooking the old North Bridge in Concord.

Open: Daily, 9 to 6 in summer, 8 to 5 in winter; closed January 1 and December 25.

WAYSIDE INN

The Wayside Inn was built prior to 1717, as there is evidence that Caleb Bull sold it at that time. In 1769, Samuel Whitney owned it. He was a member of the Provincial Assembly and muster master of the Concord Minutemen. John Winthrop lived in the inn during 1775-76, while Harvard College was located in Concord. In the 1800s the inn was owned by the Alcotts and then by the Hawthornes. Finally it was owned by Daniel Lothrop and his wife, author Margaret Sidney, whose daughter gave it to the National Park Service.

Originally the house was a saltbox of four rooms and two stories. Gradually it was enlarged.

Open: April and May, September and October, Thursday through Monday, 9 to 4:30; June through August, daily, 9 to 4:30.

Admission: Adults, nominal fee charged; children under 16, free. Guided tours are given.

WRIGHT TAVERN: Monument Square.

Ephraim Jones built the Wright Tavern in 1747 on land that was part of the Concord Common. He was from a wealthy family and was town clerk and selectman. He commanded a company of 92 men in the expedition to Nova Scotia in May, 1775.

Jones lived in the Wright Tavern for four years, selling it in 1751 to Thomas Munro, who had come to Lexington in 1730. Jones meanwhile had built the Bigelow Tavern just beyond the Main Street burying ground. There was great rivalry between the two tavernkeepers for the town's business. The selectmen got no salary in those days, but they met in a tavern and the town paid for their refreshment.

Wright Tavern did a lucrative business in rum, supplying it to the troops on training days. It was also a convenient place to stop between religious services at the meetinghouse and to gather after a funeral. It was here that the Minutemen gathered when the alarm bell sounded early on April 19, and it was here that the older men in the guard company waited while the Minutemen marched to Meriams' Corner. It was also here that the British officers Smith and Pitcairn waited while detachments of soldiers went to search the town.

Amos Wright, the landlord of 1775, came from an old Concord family. After the war the tavern was used for many kinds of meetings. In 1886 it was given to the First Parish and since then it has been run as an inn.

DANVERS

Danvers was the birthplace of the Revolutionary general Israel Putnam. This city was originally known as Salem Village, site of the 1692 witchcraft trials during which many people were tried but only 20 were executed.

REBECCA NURSE HOUSE: 149 Pine Street.
Francis Nurse built this seventeenth-century clapboard house in 1678 and named it after his wife, Rebecca. She was condemned and hanged as a witch during the witchcraft hysteria in 1692, although she maintained her innocence. The house is still furnished with period pieces.
Open: June 15 to October 15; at other times by appointment.
Admission: Nominal fee charged.

DEDHAM

Dedham dates back to 1636, when the first of its settlers arrived.

FAIRBANKS HOUSE: East Street and Easten Avenue.
Jonathan Fayerbanke brought his wife and six children to New England from Yorkshire, England, in 1633, and then to Dedham in 1636. He built his house in that year on a little knoll at the edge of a brook that flowed into the Charles River. For 270 years, his descendants lived in the house.
Jonathan's homestead, with the additions he made in 1648 and 1654, is America's most remarkable survival from the period of English settlement in the early years of the seventeenth century. It has never been extensively rebuilt. This house is of the type called a "growing house," in that the owner added to it as his prosperity and family increased. Eight generations of Fairbanks lived here.
The Fayerbanke dwelling, like other early New England houses, needed insulation, and so the spaces between the exterior and interior wood walls were filled with a variety of materials—seaweed, soft, unburned brick, and clay-daubed wattle. The brick fireplace and oven were part of the huge original brickwork.

Fairbanks House

The eleven rooms are now furnished with family heirlooms.
Open: May 1 to November 1, daily, 9 to noon and 1 to 5;
closed Mondays.
Admission: Nominal fee charged.

DEERFIELD

Deerfield was laid out in 1666 and was settled a few years
later. It became an outpost of civilization in an unknown, hos-
tile country. There were many attacks on the town, but the two
most famous were the Bloody Brook Massacre of 1675 and the
great Deerfield raid in 1704. Each time the town was rebuilt.
Many of Deerfield's eighteenth-century buildings remain today, and much of the village has been restored to its colonial
appearance. Although many of the homes are privately owned,
there are many museum houses administered by the Deerfield
Heritage Foundation. The information center is in the south
ell of Hall Tavern and is open Mondays through Saturdays from
9 to 5, and on Sundays from 1 to 5, from May through October. Shorter hours prevail during the rest of the year. There are

various combination tickets, the cost depending on the combination chosen. Guide service is offered. All Heritage Foundation houses are closed on Thanksgiving Day and from about December 15 to January 7 for the Christmas holidays.

In addition to the buildings listed here, there are a number of other houses built in the early 1800s and some shops that demonstrate various crafts. Check at the information center as to hours and admission fees for these.

ASHLEY HOUSE

Reverend Jonathan Ashley, known as an aggressive preacher, an incorrigible Loyalist, and a militant Tory, lived here from 1732, when the house was new, to 1780. The home was removed from its foundation to be used as a tobacco barn, but then was returned to its original site and restored. It exhibits antique furnishings, fabrics, pewter, china, and several possessions of the parson.

Open: Monday through Saturday 9:30 to 4:30, Sundays 1:30 to 4:30, with shorter hours during the winter.

Admission: Nominal fee charged.

DWIGHT-BERNARD HOUSE

This house, built in 1754 by Josiah Dwight, has a large kitchen with an unusual fireplace and cooking facilities. It is known for its paneled rooms and the eighteenth-century doctor's office, complete with equipment of the period. Thomas Williams and his son William Stoddard Williams lived in the house and served the community as doctors for almost 100 years.

Open: Monday through Saturday 9:30 to 4:30, Sundays 1:30 to 4:30 during the summer months; by appointment the rest of the year.

Admission: Nominal fee charged.

FRARY HOUSE

Some parts of this building were put up before 1700. It served for many years as an inn and stagecoach stop. Benedict Arnold stopped here on his way to capture Fort Ticonderoga in 1776. Frary House was the center of Whig activity during the Revolutionary War and was also the site of the first meeting of the trustees of Deerfield Academy.

Open: May 13 to November 11, Monday through Friday 9:30 to noon and 1:30 to 4:30, Sundays 1:30 to 4:30; November 12 to May 12, Monday through Saturday 10 to 3:30, Sundays 1:30 to 3:30.

Admission: Nominal fee charged.

SHELDON-HAWKS HOUSE

George Sheldon built this house in 1743 as his own residence, and it was owned by his family for 200 years. The original paneling remains today, and the sewing room has eighteenth-century fabrics.

Open: May 13 to November 11, Monday through Friday 9:30 to noon and 1:30 to 4:30, Sundays 1:30 to 4:30; November 12 to May 12, Monday through Saturday 10 to 3:30, Sundays 1:30 to 3:30.

Admission: Nominal fee charged.

WELLS-THORN HOUSE

The central section of this building was constructed about 1717 and was the home of early eighteenth-century pioneer Ebenezer Wells. By 1751 the Indian threat had passed, and Wells, a well-to-do farmer, merchant, and tavernkeeper, added the front section.

Open: May 13 to November 11, Monday through Friday 9:30 to noon and 1:30 to 4:30, Sundays 1:30 to 4:30; November to May 12, Monday through Friday 10 to 4:30, Sundays 1:30 to 3:30.

Admission: Nominal fee charged.

DORCHESTER (South Boston)

DORCHESTER HEIGHTS NATIONAL PARK: Thomas Park.

When General William Howe of the British Army looked on the redoubts that the Continental Army had built in one day, he is said to have remarked, "The rebels have done more in one night than my whole army would have done in a month."

After Ethan Allen and Benedict Arnold had captured Fort Ticonderoga in 1776, General Washington put their spoils to good use. He sent Henry Knox to drag the fort's heavy guns all the way from Lake Champlain to Boston by sledge and oxen; the presence of these weapons, coupled with the occupation of Dorchester Heights, forced General Howe to evacuate the city. By March 20, the American troops were in full possession of Boston.

The tall marble monument at the summit of the Heights looks sufficiently tall even today to reveal a position that was naturally strategic and, with fortifications, very formidable. The monument is 155 feet high, and consists of a tower and steeple reminiscent of a New England meetinghouse of 200 years ago.

OLD BLAKE HOUSE: Columbia Road and Pond Street.

Although this house was built in 1648, it contains relics not only of the colonial period but also of the Civil War. In front of the house is the Dorchester Milestone, which was erected in 1761.

DUXBURY

The second town of the Plymouth Colony, Duxbury, was the home of Elder William Brewster, Miles Standish, and John and Priscilla Alden. It was settled before 1630.

ALDEN HOUSE

In 1627, John and Priscilla Mullins Alden received a grant of land in Duxbury. There they lived during the farming season, returning to Plymouth for Sunday worship and for the winter season. In 1632, with the establishment of the church in Duxbury by Elder William Brewster, permanent settlement in Duxbury by the Aldens was accomplished.

The present John Alden House was built in 1653 by their third son, Jonathan. John and Priscilla spent their later years there with their son, who eventually died there in his eighty-ninth year.

It is believed that a kitchen, a borning room, and a buttery were added to the old house through the years. There is a powdered clam-and-oyster-shell ceiling in the great room and camber panels in the "best room." Gunstock beams are found in the chambers.

Open: June 20 through Labor Day, daily, 9:30 to 5.

Admission: Nominal fee charged.

EDGARTOWN (Martha's Vineyard)

The island of Martha's Vineyard was discovered in 1602 by Bartholomew Gosnold, an English explorer, who named the island for his daughter Martha. It immediately became popular because of its wild grapes.

THOMAS COOKE HOUSE

Thomas Cooke, collector of customs and justice of the peace, had his house erected in 1765 by shipbuilders—the slanted beams, floors, and paneling attest to this. Today it contains exhibits of scrimshaw, ship models, old china, glass, and costumes, as well as furnishings of the period.

Open: June 1 to October 1, Tuesday through Saturday 10 to 4:30, Sundays 2 to 4:30; during the rest of the year, open on Tuesdays and Wednesdays 1 to 4, Saturdays 10 to noon and 1 to 4.

Admission: Free.

GLOUCESTER

Gloucester, settled in 1623, has been famous as a fishing center since its beginnings. It is one of the oldest towns in Massachusetts.

JAMES BABSON COOPERAGE SHOP: On State Highway 127, between Gloucester and Rockport.

Here one can see an excellent exhibit of Early American tools and furniture. The building dates from 1658 and is believed to be the oldest building found on Cape Ann.

Open: July through Labor Day, daily except Mondays, 3:30 to 5:30.

Admission: Free.

SARGENT-MURRAY-GILMAN-HOUGH HOUSE: 49 Middle Street.

This Georgian house, built in 1768, contains old china, glassware, silver, and many early portraits.

Open: June 1 through September, Monday through Saturday, 11 to 4:30.

Admission: Nominal fee charged.

Interior, Sargent-Murray-Gilman-Hough House

Front entrance, hall and main staircase, Sargent-Murray-Gilman-Hough House

WHITE-ELLERY HOUSE: 274 Washington Street.

This house, featuring Early New England architecture, dates back to the mid-seventeenth century. Fine examples of pewter, pottery, and wooden utensils are on display.

Open: June 15 to September 15, daily except Mondays, 3 to 5.

Admission: Nominal fee charged.

Front Doorway, Sargent-Murray-Gilman-Hough House

HADLEY

HADLEY FARM MUSEUM: State Route 9 in the center of Hadley.

The museum is an old barn built in 1782. It contains household and farm implements of the era. Also on display are a fifteen-seat stagecoach, an old oxcart, a peddler's wagon, the first broom-making machine, and a complete smithy.

Open: May 1 to October 15, Tuesday through Saturday 10 to 4:30, Sundays 1:30 to 4:30.

Admission: Free.

PORTER-PHELPS-HUNTINGTON HOUSE: 2 miles north on State Route 47.

Moses Porter built this house in 1752 on a tract of land

known from the earliest days as "Forty Acres and its Skirts." It originally was owned in common by the householders in the northeast quarter of the stockaded town of Hadley. It was gradually acquired by the Porter family, some 500 acres becoming Moses Porter's share. The house was enlarged by Charles Phelps, an architect who married Moses Porter's only child, Elizabeth. Since 1799 it has had no structural changes. The contents of the house include a family accumulation of over 100 years.

Open: June through August, daily, 1 to 4:30; May, September, and October, weekends only, 1 to 4:30, weekdays by appointment.

Admission: Nominal fee charged.

HAVERHILL

This city was settled in 1640 on the site of the old Indian village of Pentucket. The colonial frontier town suffered many frequent Indian raids. Legend has it that in 1697 Hannah Duston was kidnapped in Haverhill by the savages, but she managed to escape and reach home safely.

BUTTONWOODS: 240 Water Street.
The Haverhill Historical Society is housed in this building. The original house was built by Nathaniel Saltonsall for himself and his bride, Elizabeth Ward, daughter of Reverend John Ward. It was damaged by fire in the late 1700s and rebuilt in 1814. Buttonwood trees planted on the grounds in 1739 give the home its name.

Open: June, July, and August, Tuesday through Saturday, 1 to 5; September to May, Tuesdays, Thursdays, and Saturdays, 2 to 5.

Admission: Nominal fee charged.

WHITTIER HOMESTEAD: 3 miles east on State Route 110.
This house, built in 1688, was the birthplace (1807) and boyhood home of John Greenleaf Whittier, who described the dwelling in his poem "Snowbound."

Open: Tuesday through Saturday 10 to 5, Sundays 1 to 5.
Admission: Nominal fee charged.

HINGHAM

OLD ORDINARY: Lincoln Street.
This building was erected before 1680 and enlarged in 1740. The taproom, kitchen, and bedroom are authentically furnished in seventeenth-century style. There is also a collection of Early American tools.
Open: June 1 through Labor Day, Tuesday through Saturday, 11:30 to 4:30.
Admission: Nominal fee charged.

OLD SHIP CHURCH (Old Ship Meetinghouse): Main Street.
It is said that this church, erected in 1681, is the oldest church in continuous use in America. It certainly is the earliest of New England's churches and is a striking survivor of seventeenth-century Massachusetts. It replaced the first meetinghouse, which had been built in 1635. Its pulpit is opposite the main door—a design developed by the Puritans in rejection of the traditional Anglican church interior.
Town meetings and religious services were held here, as well as other village gatherings, a custom that shows the close connection between politics and religion in the Puritan community.
Open: July 1 to August 31, Tuesday through Sunday, noon to 5; during the rest of the year, by appointment only.

IPSWICH

JOHN WHIPPLE HOUSE: 53 S. Main Street.
Built about 1640, the Whipple house has a steep-pitched gable roof and casement windows typical of the Elizabethan period. John Fawn, a Pilgrim settler, began construction on this site; however, he sold his property within a few years to John Whipple, who completed the building.
Sometime after 1700, the lean-to was added at the back. At the front of the house there is a seventeenth-century garden enclosed by a picket fence.
Open: April 15 through October, Tuesday through Saturday 10 to 3, Sundays 1 to 5.
Admission: Adults, nominal fee charged; children under 12, free.

LEXINGTON

BUCKMAN TAVERN

It was at Buckman Tavern that the Minutemen gathered on April 19, 1775, for the first battle of the American Revolution. The tavern was built in 1703 by Benjamin Muzzey; in 1775, it was owned by John Buckman. There still are scars on the building left by British musketballs. The building is a two-story white clapboard structure. Its eighteenth-century taproom has a large fireplace.

Open: April 19 to October 31, weekdays 10 to 5, Sundays 1 to 5.

MUNROE TAVERN: 1332 Massachusetts Avenue.

This tavern, built by William Munroe in 1695, was used as headquarters and hospital by the British on April 19, 1775. It was at this inn that George Washington was entertained at dinner in 1789. The building now contains a collection of historic articles and period furnishings.

Open: April 19 to October 31, weekdays 10 to 5, Sundays 1 to 5.

HANCOCK-CLARK HOUSE: 35 Hancock Street.

Reverend John Hancock, the patriot's grandfather, built this house in 1698. It was enlarged in 1734.

On April 18, 1775, Samuel Adams and John Hancock were sleeping on the first floor of this house when they were awakened by Paul Revere, who had ridden to Lexington to warn that the British were on the way. Hancock and Adams escaped safely to a nearby town, and the following day the American Revolution began with the clash on Lexington Green.

The house today has more than 3,000 relics of the early days of the Revolution, including Paul Revere's lantern.

Open: April 19 to November 1, weekdays 10 to 5, Sundays 1 to 5.

Admission: Nominal fee charged. There is a tour ticket for all three Lexington houses; guides are stationed at each house.

LEXINGTON GREEN: Massachusetts and Hancock streets.

Here on the morning of April 19, 1775, the short skirmish

between the Minutemen and the British forces from Boston started the American Revolution. On the east side of the Green, Henry H. Kitson's famous statue of a Minuteman stands on a pile of rocks over a stone fountain. It was erected in 1799 to commemorate the eight Minutemen who died here. Behind the monument is the tomb to which in 1835 the remains of the dead were removed from the old burying ground.

A boulder marks the site of the old belfry that called the men of Lexington to arms. Near the northwest corner another boulder marks one flank of Captain Parker's line. On it are inscribed Parker's immortal words: "Stand your ground. Don't fire unless fired upon. But if they mean to have a war, let it begin here."

MARBLEHEAD

ABBOTT HALL: Washington Square.

Here visitors can see the original deed, dated 1684, that records the purchase of the Marblehead peninsula for 16 pounds from the Indians.

Open: June through September, Monday through Friday 8 A.M. to 9 P.M., Saturdays 8 to noon, Sundays and holidays 1 to 5.

Admission: Free.

FORT SEWALL: The northeastern end of Front Street, at the harbor entrance.

Fort Sewall was built in 1742 and was manned throughout the Spanish-American War. There is an excellent view of the harbor and the Atlantic Ocean from the fort.

JEREMIAH LEE MANSION: 161 Washington Street.

This mansion is one of the surviving examples of colonial architecture that shows how the New England merchant princes lived in the eighteenth century. Colonel Jeremiah Lee came to America early in the 1700s, and by 1760 was one of the most prominent of Marblehead citizens. He built this home in 1768 in the style of a great London townhouse.

Colonel Lee owned a fleet of ships that carried cured fish to the West Indies, Portugal, and Spain. On their return the ships were laden with Cadiz salt, Madeira and Canary wine, Bilboa iron, pieces-of-eight, and West Indies molasses and sugar.

Colonel Lee's business office was in the counting room, where his private safe was built into the chimney and concealed behind a wall panel.

The three-story house is built of pine timbers and brick, over which were placed rusticated clapboards coated with limestone-gray paint mixed with sand, which gave it the appearance of masonry. It is said that Lee wanted his house to be so high that he could catch a glimpse of his sails from a glassed-in cupola on the roof as they came across the horizon.

Open: Mid-May through October 12, Monday through Saturday, 9:30 to 4.

Admission: Adults, nominal fee charged; children under 9, free.

KING HOOPER MANSION: Hooper Street.

Another merchant prince was Robert Hooper, nicknamed "King." His mansion was originally built in 1728; he enlarged it in 1745.

Open: Guided tours Tuesday through Sunday, 2 to 5.

Admission: Nominal fee charged.

OLD BURIAL HILL: Off Orner Street.

The site of Marblehead's first meetinghouse served as a cemetery during the American Revolution.

POWDER HOUSE: 37 Green Street.

This circular building of brick was built in 1755 for the storage of muskets and powder for the French and Indian War. It served the same purpose during the American Revolution and again for the War of 1812.

ST. MICHAEL'S CHURCH: Summer Street.

The material for this church was shipped from England in 1714. It is one of the oldest Episcopal churches in America. When the Declaration of Independence was announced, the bell was rung until it cracked. Paul Revere recast the bell, and it is still in use.

Open: Monday through Saturday, 9 to 5.

Admission: Free.

MARSHFIELD

WINSLOW HOUSE: Careswell Street.

Built in 1699, this house is an excellent example of early New England architecture. It is furnished with fine period pieces. Daniel Webster's law office is located on the grounds.

Open: June 1 to October 15, daily except Tuesdays, 10 to 5.

Admission: Nominal fee charged.

MEDFORD

ISAAC ROYALL HOUSE: 15 George Street.

Governor John Winthrop built a house on this site in 1637. This gave way to a more imposing brick structure in 1692. In 1732 the home was purchased by Isaac Royall, a wealthy merchant from Antigua. Although it was remodeled in 1733-37, Royall's son enlarged it again after he came into possession of it. The son was a Loyalist and fled the country after the outbreak of the Revolution.

East Facade, Isaac Royall House

The estate was confiscated and used as headquarters for General John Stark and other American officers. Generals Washington, Lee, and Sullivan were frequent visitors. After the war, the house was returned to the Royall heirs.

The house contains furnishings and wallpapers of the period. Among the historic objects displayed is one of the tea boxes dumped into Boston Harbor on the night of December 16, 1773.

Open: May 1 to October 15, daily except Mondays and Fridays, 2 to 5.

Admission: Nominal fee charged.

PETER TUFTS HOUSE: 350 Riverside Avenue.

This is one of the oldest brick houses in New England, having been built in 1678. It is an example of a seventeenth-century New England brick structure of which only eleven are known to have been built. The walls of the house, 18 inches thick, have portholes for muskets, because Indians were still a threat to the settlers when the house was built. It is strictly Georgian in design, having a central hallway with two rooms on either side of each floor.

Open: The house is open to the public throughout the year on a limited schedule. Check in advance.

NANTUCKET

The history of this island dates back to 1659, when Thomas Macy, a Puritan farmer living on the mainland, bought Nantucket Island for 30 pounds and two beaver hats. He made the purchase because he had been heavily fined for giving shelter to four Quakers during a very bad storm, and he decided to "take up his abode among savages where religious zeal had not discovered a crime in hospitality." Nantucket became one of the greatest whaling ports in the world.

JETHRO COFFIN HOUSE: Sunset Hill.

Known also as the Oldest House and the Horseshoe House, this home was built about 1686 and is one of the few extant seventeenth-century houses of Cape Cod style. It has a steeply pitched roof, a massive chimney, and small windows of the

Jethro Coffin House, Nantucket

Elizabethan period. The chimney has an inverted horseshoe in raised brick, which is supposed to ward off witches. The house now contains period furniture and china.

Open: June 15 to September 15, daily, 10 to 5.

Admission: Nominal fee charged.

Old Mill, Nantucket

OLD MILL: Mill Hill and Prospect Street.

The wood for this 1746 mill came from shipwrecks along the Atlantic coast. The mill still contains the intricate wooden machinery that was run on wind power.

Open: June 12 to September 15, Monday through Saturday.

Admission: Nominal fee charged.

NEWBURYPORT

TRISTRAM COFFIN HOUSE: 16 High School.

The first Tristram Coffin came to the colonies in 1642 with his mother, his two sisters, and his wife and five children. He was the only Loyalist to settle in the area. The house, built in 1651, was named for Tristram, Jr., a son who married in 1653. The house was enlarged and altered during the 1700s.

More than eight generations of the family lived in the house, and today it still contains their possessions. The buttery, which has been preserved, has the original churns, stools, wooden bowls, and a milkmaid's yoke.

Open: June 1 through September 1, Tuesdays, Thursdays, and Saturdays, 2 to 5; at other times by appointment; closed on holidays.

Admission: Nominal fee charged.

NORTH SWANSEA

MARTIN HOUSE: 22 Stoney Hill Road.

The Martin family lived in this house for 200 years, dating from 1728, when the home was built. Exhibits include old pewter, china, furniture, and Indian relics.

Open: May 15 to November 1, daily, 9 to 6.

Admission: Nominal fee charged.

PLYMOUTH

The Pilgrims landed at Plymouth Rock in December, 1620, and here they founded the first permanent settlement north of Virginia. Almost half the 102 persons who arrived on the *Mayflower* died of hunger and cold during the first winter.

Many of the first Pilgrims—John Alden, Miles Standish, Elder Brewster, Edward Winslow, William Bradford, and others—have been immortalized in history and literature.

At 5:00 P.M. on Fridays during the month of August and on Thanksgiving Day at 3:30 P.M., local citizens reenact the scene of the Pilgrims going to church. They climb Burial Hill, where once there was a fort, and conduct a simple service based on a description written in 1627.

Combination tickets to all Plymouth historical attractions are available at the Town Information Center, North Park, just east of U.S. 44 and State 3A, and at the Ticket to History Booth at State Pier.

Open: Mid-June to October 12, daily, 9 to 5; mid-April to mid-June and October 12 through Thanksgiving Day, Saturdays and Sundays only, 9 to 3.

Admission: Fee charged.

BURIAL HILL: Head of Town Square.

This was the site of the old fort built in 1622-23 and the watch tower built in 1643. The fort was used by the Pilgrims

Sarcophagus-First Burying Ground

both as a place of worship and for defense. Governor Bradford is buried here. There is a replica of the old powder house on the site.

COLE'S HILL: Carver Street.

Cole's Hill is still the dominant landmark of Plymouth Harbor. It rises up from the shores of Plymouth Bay near the foot of Leyden Street, the principal thoroughfare of the original settlement. Cole's Hill is traditionally considered the burial place of the colonists who died the first winter. The dead were

Pilgrim Monument

reportedly buried at night and the graves disguised to prevent the Indians from learning of the weakened state of the survivors. In later years there were cannons on the hill to ward off possible attack from the sea.

Cole's Hill

Plymouth Rock Particle

In an early assignment of land tracts, the hill became the site of the home of Deacon Samuel Fuller, the Pilgrims' "Physition & chirurgeon." It was named for a popular tavernkeeper who had many years after 1645 maintained an establishment on the hill overlooking the bay.

On the top of the bank stands a memorial to the *Mayflower* passengers and a statue of Massasoit, the Wampanoag chief whose friendship was of such value to the colony. At the foot of Cole's Hill is Plymouth Rock.

WILLIAM HARBLOW HOUSE: Sandwich and South streets.
This house, known also as the Old Fort House, was built in 1677. The furnishings illustrate the lives and industries of the Pilgrim women. Costumed hostesses demonstrate spinning, weaving, candlemaking, and other household crafts of the seventeenth century.
Open: Mid-June to mid-September, daily, 10 to 5.
Admission: Adults, nominal fee charged; children under 5, free.

JABEZ HOWLAND HOUSE: Sandwich Street.
The displays in this house, built in 1657, give visitors an idea of how the early settlers lived and worked.
Open: Daily, 10 to 5.
Admission: Nominal fee charged.

EDWARD WINSLOW HOUSE: 4 Winslow Street.
Now known as the Mayflower Society House, the structure's original section was built in 1754.
Open: June 1 to October 15, daily, 10 to 5.
Admission: Adults, nominal fee charged; children under 5, free.

JENNY GRISTMILL: Spring Lane on Town Brook.
Corn is ground today as it was at the time of the Pilgrims, in the Jenny Gristmill, the first water gristmill in the colony.
Open: May through November, daily, 9 to 6.
Admission: Adults, nominal fee charged; children under 5, free.

Jenny Gristmill

SPARROW HOUSE: 42 Summer Street.

The Plymouth Pottery occupies this house, which was built in 1640.

Open: June to mid-September, Monday through Saturday, 10 to 5; in winter, by appointment only.

Admission: Nominal fee charged.

SPOONER HOUSE: North Street.
The original furnishings are still intact in this 1749 house.
Open: June 15 to mid-October, daily, 10 to 5.
Admission: Nominal fee charged.

There are two restorations in Plymouth.

(1) *Mayflower II*: Moored at State Pier, the craft is a full-scale replica of the original *Mayflower*. Exhibits indicate how the passengers and crew lived and worked aboard the ship as

Mayflower II

she sailed across the Atlantic Ocean from England in the fall of 1620.

Open: April 1 through June 16, and September 5 through October 21, weekdays 9 to 5, weekends 9 to 5:30; June 17 through Labor Day, 9 to 8:30; October 22 through November

Plimoth Plantation House

Street Scene, Plimoth Plantation

30, 9 to 5.

Admission: Adults, nominal fee charged; children under 5, free.

(2) PLIMOTH PLANTATION: This reproduction of the Pilgrim village and fort meetinghouse is 2 miles south of Plymouth off State 3A. There are costumed guides and hostesses to demonstrate crafts and household tasks of the Pilgrims in buildings of authentic design.

Admission: Adults, nominal fee charged; children under 5, free.

QUINCY

ADAMS NATIONAL HISTORICAL SITE: 135 Adams Street.

The building on this site was home to four generations of the distinguished Adams family—from 1788 to 1927. Both President John Adams and President John Quincy Adams lived here. The house was originally built in 1731 and was enlarged at least twice. It has unusual mahogany paneling and a finely detailed staircase.

The Adams family called this "Old House." When John and Abigail Adams returned from Great Britain in 1788 and moved into the house, Abigail called it a "wren's nest." The structure was then less than half its present size.

The house has the original furnishings and the library, stable, and extensive gardens which all date back to the time of John Adams.

Open: April 19 to November 10, daily, 9 to 5.

Admission: Adults, nominal fee charged; children under 16, free when accompanied by adult.

COLONEL JOSIAH QUINCY HOUSE: 20 Muirhead Street, Wollaston.

Colonel Josiah Quincy, a prominent merchant and patriot, built this house in 1770. The 9-foot-wide central hallway leads from the front doorway to the carriage doorway at the rear. The house has impressive paneling, wainscoting, and molded cornices.

Open: June through September, Tuesdays, Thursdays, Fridays, 10 to 5; other times by appointment.
Admission: Nominal fee charged.

JOHN ADAMS BIRTHPLACE: 133 Franklin Street.

It was in this house, built in 1681, that John Adams, first vice-president and the second president of the United States, was born in 1734. He lived here until his marriage in 1764. At that time he moved into an adjacent house left to him by his father. Adams' birthplace originally consisted of two lower rooms and two upper rooms. Later two more first-floor rooms were added in a lean-to.

John Adams was a delegate to the First Continental Congress, a commissioner to France in 1777-78, a negotiator of the treaty with Britain in 1782-83, and envoy to Britain from 1785 to 1788, before he became the first vice-president of the United States.

Open: April 19 to September 30, daily except Monday, 10 to 5.
Admission: Nominal fee charged.

JOHN QUINCY ADAMS BIRTHPLACE: 141 Franklin Street.

To this house, which was originally built in 1663, John Adams and his bride Abigail moved in 1764. The sixth president of the United States, John Quincy Adams, was born here in 1767. John Adams lived here until 1783, while John Quincy Adams occupied the house from 1805 to 1807.

The building includes the law office of John Adams, the meeting place for those involved in drawing up the constitution of Massachusetts. This document was the model for other states and for the federal Constitution.

The house originally consisted of two upper and two lower rooms, but two more lower rooms were added when a kitchen lean-to was built.

Open: April 19 to September 30, daily except Monday, 10 to 5.
Admission: Nominal fee charged; combined admission to both Adams houses is available.

QUINCY HOMESTEAD: 34 Butler Road.

This house was the birthplace of Dorothy Quincy, who became the wife of John Hancock. It was built in 1680.

Open: April 18 through October 31, daily except Monday, 10 to 5.

Admission: Nominal fee charged.

SALEM

Salem, founded in 1626, was the capital of the Massachusetts Bay Colony until 1630. Salem was the scene in 1692 of the notorious witchcraft trials. By the time the American Revolution was ended, Salem had become a prosperous shipping center.

CHARTER STREET BURYING GROUND

Among the markers here is a stone which reads, "Mr. Nathaniel Mather, deceased October 17, 1688, an aged person that has seen but nineteen Winters in the World."

ESSEX INSTITUTE: 123 Essex Street.

One of the largest collections in the United States of antiquarian and historical objects is housed here. There are a number of buildings in Salem that are part of the institute.

Open: Tuesday through Saturday 9 to 4:30, Sundays and holidays 2 to 5; closed Mondays, January 1, July 4, Thanksgiving Day, December 25.

Admission: Free. A combination ticket for the houses is available.

CROWNINSHIELD-BENTLEY HOUSE: 126 Essex Street.

This dwelling was built by John Crowninshield, a fish merchant and sea captain, in 1727, the year his twin daughters were born. Crowninshield was the son of German-born physician Johannes Caspar Richter von Cronenshilt.

When Captain John Crowninshield died in 1761, there was a five-year lapse before the estate was settled. His widow, Antis Crowninshield, was given the "Western part of the Mansion House . . . with the yard and land adjoining." The division ran right through the middle of the front door and entryway beyond. It included for the widow a "Privilege of one-half of the Stir Way and the Western Part of the cellar as it is not petitioned off." A son Jacob and his wife Hannah fell heir to the eastern part of the house. It remained so divided until 1832. The two-and-one-half-story house contains furnishings of the eighteenth century.

Open: June through October 15, Tuesday through Saturday 10 to 4, Sundays and holidays 2 to 4:30; closed Mondays and July 4. Guided tours.

Admission: Adults, nominal fee charged; children under 12, free if accompanied by adults.

JOHN WARD HOUSE: 132 Essex Street.

This two-and-one-half-story structure originally included only the western half of the present house when it was built in 1684. It consisted of the parlor and its chamber above, the brick chimney, porch, and stairways. The house has an overhang at both the front and west ends, which gives additional space to the bedroom on the second story. At some later date the hall, the large fireplace, and upstairs chamber were added. The lean-to contains an apothecary shop and a weaving loom of the early nineteenth century.

Open: June to October 15, Tuesday through Saturday 10 to 4, Sundays and holidays 2 to 4:30; closed July 4. Guided tours available.

Admission: Adults, nominal fee charged; children under 12, free if accompanied by adults.

PEIRCE NICHOLS HOUSE: 60 Federal Street.

Samuel McIntire, a prominent architect, built this house in 1782 for Jerathmeel Peirce, a wealthy East Indian merchant.

The house has a balustraded roof deck so that Peirce could look out across the bay for the tall sails of his ships coming in from China. It has its original furnishings and a counting house.

Open: Tuesday through Saturday, 2 to 4:30; closed Sundays, Mondays, and holidays. Guided tours available.

Admission: Adults, nominal fee charged; children under 12, free if accompanied by adults.

House of Seven Gables

HOUSE OF SEVEN GABLES: 54 Turner Street.

Erected in 1668 and originally known as the Captain John Turner House, this home was built to face south across the harbor when the Puritan settlement was only forty-two years old. At the time it had only four gables, but when Turner added a wing in 1678 the seven gables resulted.

The house then went to the captain's son, John Turner II, who is believed to have put in secret stairs in the huge central chimney for the protection of his sister when Salem's notorious witch hangings occurred in 1692. Nathaniel Hawthorne used the house for the setting of his novel *The House of the Seven Gables;* the name for the house has remained ever since.

There are a number of other buildings on the grounds—the old bakery, Hathaway House (1682), Retire Beckett House (1655), and the Hawthorne House where Nathaniel Hawthorne was born in 1804.

Open: July 1 to Labor Day, daily 9:30 to 7:30; Labor Day to June 30, daily 10 to 4:45; closed Thanksgiving Day, Christmas, and New Year's Day.

Admission: Nominal fee charged.

THE PIONEER'S VILLAGE: Forest River Park.

This village is a reproduction of the 1630 settlement. There are sod-roofed dugouts of palisaded logs, barked-covered wigwams, pine cottages, thatch-roofed houses, a pillory, and stocks. Typical Puritan gardens have been created, and the homes contain the furnishings, cooking utensils, and other equipment of those days as well as tools used for salt making, fish flaking, and log sawing.

Open: June 1 through Labor Day, daily 9:30 to 6:30; Labor Day through October 12, daily 10 to 5; October 12 to October 31 by appointment.

Admission: Nominal fee charged.

ROPES MANSION: 318 Essex Street.

Built in 1719 by a wealthy Salem merchant, it is furnished with four generations of Ropes family items.

Open: May to October 31, Monday through Saturday, 10 to 4:30; closed holidays.

Admission: Nominal fee charged; admission to gardens, free.

SALEM MARITIME NATIONAL HISTORIC SITE: 178 Derby Street.

The site includes the Old Custom House, Derby Wharf, Derby House, and the Old Rum Shop.

DERBY MANSION: In 1761, Captain Richard Derby began construction of a brick mansion two blocks west of the famous House of the Seven Gables, within sight of the long stone wharf he built about the same time. The house was a wedding present for his son, Elias Haskell Derby, who is said to have become America's first millionaire when he and his father opened new trade routes to the Orient with their fleet of ships. The Derbys fitted out 85 privateers during the Revolution.

The house is furnished to reflect the living conditions of a successful merchant.

Open: Guided tours daily, 9:30 to 4:30; closed January 1, Thanksgiving Day, and December 25.

Admission: Adults, nominal fee charged; children under 16, free.

WITCH HOUSE: 310½ Essex Street.

Jonathan Corwin, one of the witchcraft judges, had this house built for him in 1692. It was also the site of some of the preliminary witchcraft examinations.

Open: May 1 to October 1, daily 10 to 6; March 1 to May 1, and October 31 to December 31 by appointment.

Admission: Nominal fee charged.

SAUGUS

The Saugus ironworks were begun in 1646. The ironworks set up here gave the world its first true cast iron and wrought iron production, serving as the beginning of the American iron and steel industry.

IRONWORKS

This is a reconstruction of the seventeenth-century ironworks which operated intermittently between 1648 and 1670. The works consisted of a blast furnace, casting house, a rolling and slitting mill, and a forge. It originally was called the Company of Undertakers for the Iron Works in England and used to construct ironworks under the direction of Richard Leader. John Winthrop, Jr. was one of the partners.

The works not only produced crude pig iron and cast ware but its forge manufactured bars of wrought iron, from which could be made the tools and hardware that were needed by colonial farms and enterprises. Its rolling and slitting mill turned out rod iron that could be shaped into nails, a much needed commodity in the colonies. Eventually the business failed in 1670, but the migration of its workers to other parts of the colonies made it an important link in the iron and steel industry.

Not only is this a full-scale model of the original seventeenth-century works, but in the museum can also be seen articles uncovered in the excavation.

Open: April through October 9, daily 9 to 5; October 10 through March, 9 to 4.

Admission: Adults, nominal fee charged; children under 16, free.

OLD IRONMASTER'S HOUSE

This was the home of the first proprietor of the Saugus Ironworks and was built in 1648. It features 10-foot fireplaces and hand-hewn beams and contains a collection of Early American furnishings and utensils.

SCOTCH-BOARDMAN HOUSE: 17 Howard Street.

Much of the original finish of this building is unspoiled. Some say that it was built by Oliver Cromwell to shelter Scottish prisoners captured in the Battle of Dunbar, Scotland, in 1650 and then transported to America. However, it is generally believed that the house was built after 1686, since it follows the plan of a typical family dwelling of the period. The structure has the usual two-room, central chimney plan, is two-and-one-half stories high, and has a half cellar. A lean-to was added later on.

The house is open to the public in the summer.

SOMERVILLE

OLD POWDER HOUSE

Originally built as a gristmill about 1704, in 1775 the building became a magazine of the American Army besieging Boston. The walls are two feet thick, with an inner structure of brick and an outer layer of a blue stone that probably was quarried nearby. Many people consider this building to be one of the finest antique relics in the state.

Open: Check locally.
Admission: Check locally.

STOCKBRIDGE

This town was set up originally as an Indian mission in 1734. Reverend John Sergeant taught and preached to the Stockbridge Indians in their own language, until his death in 1749. His successor was Reverend Jonathan Edwards.

MISSION HOUSE: Main Street.

Built in 1739 for Reverend John Sergeant, the house is now an Early American museum.

Open: Memorial Day to Labor Day, Tuesday through Saturday 10 to 5, Sundays and holidays 11 to 4; Labor Day to October 15, Saturdays and Sundays only.

Admission: Nominal fee charged.

STURBRIDGE

OLD STURBRIDGE VILLAGE: Junction of the Massachusetts Turnpike, I-86, U.S. 20, and State 131.

A recreated New England village in which are found the homes, shops, general store, schoolhouse, tavern, meetinghouse, pillory, and stocks of a typical New England country town of the late 1700s. Craftsmen demonstrate the various crafts and household tasks of the time. Picnic areas and a restaurant are

Scene of Old Sturbridge Village

Scene of Old Sturbridge Village

also on the grounds.

Open: April through October, daily, 9:30 to 5:30; November through March, daily, 10 to 4; closed January 1 and December 25.

Admission: Adults, fee charged; children under 6, free.

TOPSFIELD

PARSON CAPEN HOUSE: Off Village Green.

The Parson Capen House is considered to be one of the finest surviving English colonial dwellings in the United States. Except for the clapboards in place of the half-timbers, the house is a faithful copy of the English manor house of the seventeenth century. It was built for Reverend Joseph Capen, minister at Topsfield, on a 12-acre plot given to him by the town in 1682.

There is one room at either side of the massive central brick fireplace. A central winding staircase is built against the chimney. Furnishings are of the seventeenth century and include a good hutch, which has been called unique in America, and a baluster-back armchair inscribed "P. Capen 1708," believed to have been part of the wedding furniture of Priscilla Capen, the parson's daughter.

Open: June 15 to September 15, daily, 1 to 4:30; other times by appointment.

Admission: Nominal fee charged.

WATERTOWN

ABRAHAM BROWNE HOUSE: 562 Main Street.

This house was built about 1698 by Captain Abraham Browne and was kept in the family until 1897. It has one of the few original three-part casement window frames known to exist in New England.

Open: June through October, Mondays, Wednesdays, and Fridays, 2 to 5; at other times by appointment.

Admission: Nominal fee charged.

WEST SPRINGFIELD

OLD DAY HOUSE: 70 Park Street.

Josiah Day built this brick saltbox house in 1754, and his descendants lived in it until 1902. It is furnished with antiques of the 1700s.

Open: Wednesday through Sunday, 1 to 5; closed holidays.

Admission: Nominal fee charged.

STORROWTOWN VILLAGE: On State 147, 1 mile west of U.S. 5, on Exposition Grounds.

A restored early American village with various homes, craft shops, and a schoolhouse.

Open: June 18 through Labor Day, Monday through Saturday, 1 to 5; guides available.

Admission: Adults, nominal fee charged; children under 12, free.

WENHAM

CLAFLIN-RICHARDS HOUSE
Records show that Robert Mack Claflin lived here in 1661. In 1673 the town built an addition on the house for Pastor Gerrish, when Claflin moved into another house. On display are period furniture, kitchen utensils, quilts, and needlework.

Open: Monday through Friday, 1 to 4; closed holidays and during the month of February.

Admission: Nominal fee charged.

YARMOUTHPORT

CAPTAIN BANGS HALLETT HOUSE: On Strawberry Lane.
This restored eighteenth-century house, furnished in the period, contains exhibits including children's toys, projectile points, and scrimshaw.

Open: June 30 through September, Monday through Saturday, 2 to 3; closed Sundays and holidays.

Admission: Adults, nominal fee charged; children under 12, free.

COLONEL JOHN THATCHER HOUSE: State 6A.
The original part of the house was built in 1680. It contains Early American antiques.

Open: June through September, Tuesday through Saturday, 11 to 4; closed Sundays and holidays.

Admission: Nominal fee charged.

WINSLOW CROCKER HOUSE: On State 6A.
This house, built in 1780, features unusual woodwork in the eighteenth-century manner.

Open: June through September, Tuesday through Saturday, 11 to 4; at other times by appointment.

Admission: Nominal fee charged.

Connecticut

HISTORY

The first settlers of Connecticut were colonists who objected to the rigid laws of Massachusetts. They established the first English settlement, in 1634, in Wethersfield; this was soon followed by the settlements of Windsor and Hartford. In 1639 the three towns drew up the "Fundamental Orders of Connecticut," which decreed that there would be no religious requirement for citizenship, although the church had strict control over the government.

In 1662, after fifteen towns had been settled, Connecticut secured a charter from King Charles II extending the boundaries of the Connecticut colony to include a number of small settlements along Long Island Sound. The charter also gave the settlers the right to govern themselves.

In 1686, Sir Edmund Andros, governor of New York, was appointed governor general of the dominion of New England, and all previous charters were declared void. However, the "Hartford three" would not surrender their charter and allegedly hid it in what became known as the Charter Oak.

Andros ruled until the accession of William III in 1689, when the New England charters were again deemed valid. The Connecticut charter of 1662 was kept as the state charter even after the state won its independence from Great Britain in the Revolutionary War.

There were only four battles fought on Connecticut soil during the Revolution. In one of these battles, Benedict Arnold led the British into New London, burned the wharves and stores, then crossed the river to Groton and massacred the garrison at Fort Griswold. More than 30,000 Connecticut men were in the Continental Army; it has been estimated that in 1776 about one-half of George Washington's New York City forces came from Connecticut.

BETHEL

PUTNAM MEMORIAL STATE PARK: Between Bethel and Redding Ridge on State 58.

During the winter of 1778-79, General Israel Putnam quartered his New England troops here. The blockhouse and palisades have been restored and there are traces of other buildings. A colonial museum in the park houses Revolutionary relics.

Open: Memorial Day to Labor Day, daily, noon to 4.

Admission: Free.

COS COB

BUSH-HOLLY HOUSE: 39 Strickland Road, near Greenwich.

This saltbox, originally built in 1686, is furnished with period pieces. There is a collection of John Rogers plaster sculptures in a separate building.

Open: Summer, Tuesday through Saturday 10 to noon and 2 to 5, Sundays 2 to 4; in winter, Tuesday through Saturday 10 to 4, Sundays 2 to 4.

Admission: Nominal fee charged.

COVENTRY

NATHAN HALE HOMESTEAD: South Street.

This home was built in 1776 by the father of Nathan Hale, the Revolutionary spy who was captured and hanged by the British on September 22, 1776. Nathan Hale never saw the finished house, since he was executed one month prior to its completion. There had been an older dwelling in which Hale had been born on June 6, 1755, but that was pulled down after the new house was erected. Local legend has it that a part of the ell of the present house is a remnant of the original birthplace structure.

The house, which shows some outstanding woodwork detail, has been restored and furnished with possessions of the Hale family.

Open: May 15 to October 15, daily, 1 to 5.

Admission: Nominal fee charged.

EAST GRANBY

NEWGATE PRISON AND SIMSBURY COPPER MINES

The Simsbury mines were reportedly the first copper mines developed in British America, a company being established in 1707 to extract their ore. "Granby coppers" were coins in common use for many years. However, by the year 1773 the work at the mines had virtually ceased, since the shipping of

Old New Gate Prison

Old New Gate Prison

ore to England for smelting was too expensive.

In 1773, the mine caverns were made into a prison and were named after the notorious Newgate prison in London. During the Revolution it was used to house Tories and prisoners of war.

The copper caves still survive, although the prison structures, dating mostly from the early nineteenth century, are in ruins.

Open: Memorial Day through October, Tuesday through Sunday, 10 to 4:30.

Admission: Nominal fee charged.

Underground Dungeons at Old New Gate Prison

EAST LYME

THOMAS LEE HOUSE

Considered to be the oldest frame house in Connecticut, this structure was probably built by Thomas Lee II. Widow Lee had married Greenleaf Larrabee and settled in Norwich in 1660.

The Lee family occupied an important position in the life of the colony. Thomas Lee II served as constable and held a seat in the General Assembly in 1676; he also owned a considerable amount of land. Thomas Lee was justice of peace for more than forty years and used the house as his office.

The house was moved in 1713 when a new road was put through. The most unusual feature in the house is a casement window in the south wall of the west chamber—one of two such casements found in Connecticut.

The house is an excellent example of early colonial architecture and is furnished in period style.

Open: Memorial Day to October 12, daily except Tuesdays, 10 to 5.

Admission: Nominal fee charged.

ESSEX

PRATT HOUSE: 20 West Avenue.

A fine collection of Early American furnishings is exhibited in the house, believed to have been built in 1725.

Open: Monday through Friday 1 to 4; Saturdays, Sundays, and holidays by appointment only.

Admission: Nominal fee charged.

FARMINGTON

STANLEY-WHITMAN HOUSE: 37 High Street.

This home, built around 1660 by John Stanley, was bought in 1735 by Reverend Samuel Whitman, minister in Farmington from 1706 to 1751. The house is believed to be one of the earliest and best preserved of the framed overhang type in Connecticut. It is an almost perfect example of the added lean-to house, of the Elizabethan or Jacobean architecture that was brought from England by the early settlers. The framed front

Stanley-Whitman House

overhang projects 1½ feet beyond the first floor and serves no utilitarian purpose.

The interior is typical of the early central chimney plan. The great chimney was made mostly of flat fieldstone, laid in clay mixed with straw, in the old English fashion.

The lean-to at the rear of the house was added about 1760 and includes the kitchen, a buttery room at one end, and the traditional "birth and death" room at the other.

At the rear of the house a wing has been added for exhibits of old manuscripts, maps, costumes, china, and musical instruments. There is also a wagon shed on the grounds housing early farm implements. The garden at the back contains about thirty varieties of the herbs and scented geraniums typical of colonial gardens.

Open: April 1 to November 30, Tuesday through Saturday 10 to noon and 2 to 5, Sundays 2 to 5; December 1 to March 31, Fridays and Saturdays 10 to noon and 2 to 5, Sundays 2 to 5.

Admission: Nominal fee charged.

GREENWICH

PUTNAM COTTAGE: 24 East Putnam Avenue.

In 1692, Thomas Knapp purchased this property fronting on the post road, the direct stagecoach route between New York and Boston. At that time the building was known as Knapp's Tavern.

During the Revolutionary War the structure was owned by Captain Israel Knapp and was still run as a tavern. It was here in 1779 that General Israel Putnam escaped from the British.

Hand-hewn beams were found in the living room when the house was restored. The corners of the room were made of actual tree trunks. There is a magnificent fieldstone fireplace supported by huge, hand-hewn oak beams. The house now exhibits Revolutionary and other historical relics.

Open: Mondays, Thursday through Saturday, 10 to 4.

Admission: Adults, nominal fee charged; children under 12, free.

Putnam Cottage, Greenwich, Conn.

GROTON

FORT GRISWOLD STATE PARK

This area was the scene of a massacre in 1781 when British forces, led by Benedict Arnold, took the fort and burned the towns of New London and Groton. On the grounds are the Monument House and the Groton Monument.

MONUMENT HOUSE

This house contains relics of the Fort Griswold massacre as well as china and furniture of the period.

Open: Memorial Day to Labor Day, Tuesday through Sunday, 1 to 4.

GROTON MONUMENT

This monument, located on the hilltop near Fort Griswold, is 135 feet high and contains the names of the victims of the 1781 massacre.

Open: Memorial Day to Labor Day, daily, 8:30 to 11:30 and 1 to 4; Labor Day to Columbus Day, daily except Mondays, 8:30 to 11:30 and 1 to 4.

GUILFORD

THOMAS GRISWOLD HOUSE MUSEUM: 171 Boston Street.

This colonial saltbox, believed to have been built in 1735, is furnished in period style. In a barn behind the house is an early blacksmith shop, complete with forge and ox sling, as well as hundreds of farm utensils and agricultural tools.

Open: April 1 through November 20, Tuesday through Sunday, 11 to 5.

Admission: Adults, nominal fee charged; children under 12, free.

HYLAND HOUSE: 84 Boston Street.

The original house was built by George Hyland in 1660 as a two-story, four-room house. Ebeneezer Parmalee bought it about 1720 and added a lean-to and the present front staircase. The house is furnished in seventeenth-century style.

Open: June 14 to September 30, daily, 10 to 5.

Admission: Adults, nominal fee charged; children under 12, free.

HENRY WHITFIELD STATE HISTORICAL MUSEUM: Whitfield Street.

In 1639, Reverend Henry Whitfield brought his flock to settle in Guilford. Whitfield had broken with the Church of England and had brought to America families from his congregation in the town of Ockley and from neighboring congregations in Surrey and Kent. They landed at Quinnipiac (New Haven), where Whitfield's friend John Davenport had established a colony. They bought more land from the Indians for their town half-way between Quinnipiac and Saybrook, where another friend of Whitfield's, George Fenwick, had settled.

Reverend Whitfield and his congregation, beginning in the fall of 1639, built a stone house on a knoll at the edge of Long Island Sound. Today that building is believed to be the oldest stone dwelling erected by white men within the present boun-

Henry Whitfield House

daries of the United States.

The house not only served as a meetinghouse and a fort for the twenty-five families who had accompanied him, but also as a home for his wife Dorothy, seven of their nine children, and whatever servants they had. It is an L-shaped house almost 40 feet long in each wing, two stories high, topped by a steeply pitched roof that covered a spacious attic. Its stone walls are 2 feet thick.

The building is furnished with seventeenth-century antiques. Exhibits include weaving equipment, an herb garden, and a clock made in Guilford in 1726.

Open: April to November, daily except Mondays and Tuesdays, 10 to 5; November to April, Wednesday through Sunday, 10 to 4; closed December 15 to January 15 and on holidays.

Admission: Adults, nominal fee charged; children under 12, free.

HARTFORD

It was at the Council Chamber in Hartford that Sir Edmund Andros, governor general of the Dominion of New England, demanded the colony's charter. Joseph Wadsworth escaped with the charter, which he hid in a hollow oak tree, since known as the Charter Oak.

HARTFORD *Courant*: 285 Broad Street.

The oldest newspaper in America with a continuous name and circulation was founded here in 1764. Israel Putnam was the *Courant*'s war correspondent and George Washington was a subscriber.

AMOS BULL HOUSE: 350 Main Street.

This is one of the few houses still standing in Hartford that was built in the 1700s. It probably stood originally on a narrow lot with houses on either side as there are no side windows on the first two floors.

The plain, regularly spaced second-floor windows on the front appear to be the original ones, as do the three dormers above them. Some of the second-floor interior, such as the paneled wainscoting, cornices, and fireplace trim, are believed

Amos Bull House

to be original.

The first owner of the house was Amos Bull, who operated a dry goods business which he sold around 1820; since then it has had several uses.

Open: Check locally.

LEBANON

JONATHAN TRUMBULL WAR OFFICE: West Town Street. This simple frame building is supposed to have been the headquarters from which Governor Jonathan Trumbull sent supplies to the Continental Army. The structure was originally a store, built about 1732 by Joseph Trumbull, father of Jonathan. The office stood next to the Trumbull home, but when both buildings were moved, the office was placed across Lebanon Commons from the home.

The store became known as the War Office because in the back room Governor Trumbull presided over meetings of the Council of Safety and of the General Assembly.

GOVERNOR JONATHAN TRUMBULL HOUSE

Governor Jonathan Trumbull's son John, best known for his paintings of leaders and dramatic scenes of the Revolutionary War, was born here. The house was built by Joseph Trumbull sometime between 1737 and 1740 as a home for his son Jonathan and his wife, Faith Robinson.

The building is remarkable for the construction of its chimneys, whose open spaces provided secret escape passages into the attic. The governor hid in one of these passages when there was a price set on his head because of his patriotism.

Jonathan Trumbull held nearly every public office in the state, from the age of 23, when he was first elected to the General Assembly of Connecticut, until he was chosen governor in 1769. He was in frequent conferences with General Washington, Benjamin Franklin, Samuel and John Adams, Thomas Jefferson, the Marquis de Lafayette, and Count de Rochambeau.

The house displays many original manuscripts.

Open: May through November 1, Tuesday through Saturday, 1 to 6.

Admission: Adults, nominal fee charged; children, free.

WASHINGTON STABLE: Adjacent to the Governor Jonathan Trumbull Homestead.

This stable was removed from North Hartford to Lebanon in 1954. During visits to Hartford, General George Washington would quarter his favorite horse, Nelson, in this stable. It was this gray horse that he rode on September 21, 1780, when he met with Colonel Jeremiah Wadsworth, Marquis de Lafayette, and Count Jean Baptiste de Rochambeau in his house across from the stable, when they laid plans for the victory at Yorktown. The stable houses many relics of Revolutionary times—oxcarts, wagons, and the Newcomb collection of early ironware.

LITCHFIELD

TAPPING REEVE HOUSE AND LAW SCHOOL: South Street between the Green and Wolcott Avenue.

The house was built in 1772 by Judge Tapping Reeve, who in 1784 erected another building next to it to house the first law school in the United States. Many of the men who studied under Tapping Reeve became prominent lawyers, judges, and politicians, and the school is known to have influenced the development of American law. Some of its graduates were Vice-Presidents Aaron Burr and John C. Calhoun, three justices of the United States Supreme Court, ninety members of the House of Representatives, and twenty-six senators.

Open: May 15 to October 15; check hours locally as they are constantly changing.

Admission: Nominal fee charged.

MADISON

NATHANIEL ALLIS HOUSE: 853 Boston Post Road (U.S. 1).

The house was built around 1739 by Nathaniel Allis II. It was

Nathaniel Allis House

Nathaniel Allis House

originally a one-story building of four rooms; later on a second story was built and extra rooms added in the back, and in 1860 still more rooms were added.

The house has four corner fireplaces and contains many interesting pieces of furniture. There is a carriage house in the rear that features displays of early farm tools, looms, and Indian artifacts.

Open: June 15 to September 15, daily except Sundays and Mondays, 10 to 5.

Admission: Adults, nominal fee charged; children under 12, free.

MYSTIC

MYSTIC SEAPORT: Along the Mystic River on State Route 27.

This historical seaport restoration includes museums housing many varied marine exhibits. A wooden whaling ship and several other vessels are exhibited at the wharves. Many crafts are demonstrated.

Open: Daily except December 25, 10 to 4.

Admission: Fee charged; prices highest from mid-April to mid-November.

DENISON HOMESTEAD: Pequot-Sepos Road.

In the latter part of the seventeenth century, Captain George Denison, veteran of Cromwell's Army, brought his wife and four children to America. He was granted 200 acres of hill, valley, brook, and field, a few miles east of New London. There he built a crude home surrounded by a stockade on the heights overlooking the Pequotsepos, a small river that meandered through the meadow to Fisher's Island Sound.

In 1717 his grandson, George Denison III, built the house that is still standing today. It was a typical four-square, center chimney saltbox. Later the roof was raised to make two full stories at the rear of the house. There is a rare trimmer arch over the kitchen fireplace supporting a hearthstone above.

The furnishings are all authentic and were used by the Denison family up to 1900.

Open: April 15 to November 1, Tuesday through Sunday, 1 to 5.

Admission: Adults, nominal fee charged; children under 12, free.

WHITEHALL MANSION: Junction of I-95 and State Route 27.

This is a restored pre-Revolutionary house with colonial furnishings.

Open: May 1 through October 15, Monday through Friday and Sundays, 2 to 4.

Admission: Nominal fee charged.

NEW CANAAN

HANFORD-SILLIMAN HOUSE

This example of Georgian architecture was built about 1764. It features a great central chimney, hand-forged nails, and considerable wood carving. There also is a studio built by John Rogers which houses an extensive collection of his work.

Open: Year round, Tuesdays, Thursdays, Saturdays, and Sundays, 2 to 4:30.

Admission: Free.

Hanford-Silliman House

NEW HAVEN

The Puritans who designed New Haven divided it into nine equal squares, the central square being reserved for the public. From 1701 to 1875, New Haven and Hartford were the joint capitals of Connecticut.

CONNECTICUT HALL: Bounded by High, Chapel, Elm, and College streets.

Connecticut Hall is Yale University's only pre-Revolutionary building, being the lone survivor of "Brick Room," a group of brick buildings erected in the Georgian style. The hall was built between 1750 and 1752 and is located on the "Old Campus." It is three stories high, topped by a gambrel roof. In 1796, dormer windows and another story were added. The interior was completely redone in 1954, and the building is now used for faculty rooms, seminars, and refreshment rooms.

PARDEE MORRIS HOUSE: 325 Lighthouse Road.

Although this house was built in 1685, it was partially

destroyed during the Revolution and was rebuilt in 1780. At the time of the rebuilding, there was only a portion of the early house remaining. A ballroom was added later.

The house has stone ends laid up in a mortar of oyster shells. There are various roof levels, eight fireplaces, a vaulted ball-room, and a vast beamed basement kitchen. The furnishings are of the period.

Open: May to October 31, Monday through Friday, 10 to 5; closed weekends and holidays.

Admission: Donations.

NEW LONDON

New London was founded at the mouth of the Thames River in 1646 by a group of Puritan families under John Winthrop, the younger. It served as the principal port for privateers during the Revolution, and therefore was one of the main objectives of Benedict Arnold's Tory forces in 1781. Most of the wharves and stores were burned by the attackers, who were assisted by a 32-vessel British fleet.

JOSHUA HEMPSTED HOUSE: 11 Hempstead Street.

Joshua Hempsted was not the first of his name in New London, but the house he built in 1678 and the diary his son Joshua II kept from 1711 until 1758 reveal a great deal about the community the first Hempsted, Robert, helped to found in 1646.

The Hempsted land was at first a 14-acre farm, well outside the town and only a quarter of a mile from water. Today it is in the heart of New London, a mile or more from the deep harbor. A brook that ran by the door is buried deep in a culvert.

Joshua II was a shipwright, carpenter, politician, gravestone engraver, and farmer who kept a diary so detailed that, when the house was restored, even the sliding diamond-paned case-ment windows in the second floor bedroom could be recon-structed according to his notes.

Hempsted House, like many in seventeenth-century New England, was built in stages. At first it had just one big room on each floor to the right of the immense chimney. Joshua later added two lean-tos. The walls are shingled on vertical boarding

Hempsted House

---

and filled with seaweed for insulation.

Nathan Hale was a friend of Stephen Hempsted, its owner during the days of the American Revolution, and was a frequent visitor here.

In 1781, when Benedict Arnold burned New London, the Hempsted farm was probably spared because it was still on the outskirts of the town.

Open: May 15 to October 15, daily except Mondays, 1 to 4.
Admission: Nominal fee charged.

OLD TOWN MILL: Main and Mill streets.

Governor Winthrop built the town's gristmill about 1650; it was rebuilt in 1712. The original waterwheel is still in place.

Open: June 1 to September 14, Tuesday through Sunday, 12:30 to 5.
Admission: Free.

SHAW MANSION: 11 Blinman Street.

Captain Nathaniel Shaw, a wealthy shipowner, built this house in 1756. It is said that he built it partly to give employment to a band of Acadian refugees. The eaves of both the gabled main house and its big four-square wing are elegantly balustraded.

Washington once stayed in the mansion. During the Revolution, the house was set on fire, but was saved by some barrels that had been stored in the attic—as the barrels burst, their contents, vinegar, came pouring down onto the lower floors and put out the flames.

Open: Daily except January, 1 to 4.

Admission: Donation.

NORWICH

LEFFINGWELL INN: 348 Washington Street, junction of State Routes 2, 32, and 169.

One of the original settlers of Norwich (1659) was William Backus, Sr., whose son inherited this property and in 1675 built a house on the lot. Later this was sold to Ensign Thomas Leffingwell. In 1701, Leffingwell was granted a license to "Keep a publique house of entertainment for strangers." The house became very popular as an inn.

Norwich in 1776 was one of the twelve largest cities in the entire thirteen colonies and was the center of vigorous support for the move for independence. Christopher Leffingwell, who owned the inn at the time, was an ardent patriot. By 1770 he had established the first paper mill in Connecticut, a stocking factory, a pottery, a chocolate mill, fulling mill, clothier's shop, and dye house. He became one of the most dependable sources of supply for the Continental Army.

Many Revolutionary War conferences were held in the Tavern Room of the inn, since the windows were heavily shuttered and offered the needed privacy.

The 1675 bedroom has been restored and equipped with seventeenth- and eighteenth-century furnishings. In the basement are displays of antique dolls, Norwich silver, and Indian artifacts.

Open: May 16 to October 15, Tuesday through Sunday, 2 to 4; June 1 through Labor Day, Tuesday through Sunday, 10 to 12:30; October 16 to May 16, Saturdays and Sundays only, 2 to 4.

Admission: Adults, nominal fee charged; children under 12, free.

OLD SAYBROOK

Saybrook Parish was settled in 1623 by the Dutch and in 1635 by the English. Until 1716, Yale College, founded in 1701, was located here.

SIMSBURY

SIMSBURY HISTORIC CENTER: 800 Hopmeadow Street.

These grounds contain an eighteenth-century house, a one-room schoolhouse, an herb garden, carriage house, meeting-house, and a tool shed.

Open: May to November, Tuesday through Saturday, 1 to 4; during the rest of the year, by appointment only.

Admission: Adults, nominal fee charged; children 12 and under, free when accompanied by adult.

STAMFORD

On July 1, 1640, Captain Nathaniel Turner of Quinnipiac, New Haven Colony, purchased land from the Indians. The next year a group of people in Wetherfield decided to emigrate and form a new settlement. They obtained from the colony of New Haven the right to the land for thirty-three pounds. In the spring of 1641, twenty-eight men and their families founded the new settlement, which they called Rippowam. In 1642 they changed the name to Stamford.

HOYT FARM HOUSE: 713 Bedford Street.

Although it was a farm in 1699, today the Hoyt House stands in downtown Stamford and is the only example of seventeenth-century architecture in the city. The Stamford Historical Society uses the structure as its headquarters.

Joshua Hoyt was granted a lot at the town meeting held on February 24, 1668. He left it to his son Samuel, who built the farm house about 1699.

Hoyt Farm House

Open: By appointment only.
Admission: Donation.

STRATFORD

JUDSON HOUSE AND MUSEUM: 967 Academy Hill.
This house, built in 1723 by Captain David Judson, features

Judson House

construction typical of many seventeenth- and eighteenth-century New England homes. The museum houses exhibits from all periods of Stratford's history.

Open: May through November, Wednesdays, Saturdays, and Sundays, 11 to 5.

Admission: Nominal fee charged.

SUFFIELD

HATHAWAY HOUSE: Main Street, State 75.

Abraham Burbank built this house sometime after he bought the property in 1735. It is believed that Burbank did not live in this clapboard dwelling until 1760, seven years before his death. The house originally had four rooms—two on each side of the two floors, fireplaces in each one, all sharing the central chimney.

When Oliver Phelps moved to Suffield in 1788, he bought the finest house in the town—the one that Abraham Burbank had built. He added a north wing, used the latest designs in English paneling for the interior, and purchased the most fashionable French wallpapers he could find.

Oliver Phelps wanted to make an impression on the town. He had left as a poor boy, following the completion of his indentured service to a local merchant. He worked hard—first as a peddler in the Massachusetts countryside selling wooden dishes and later as a trader. He eventually became one of the nation's largest landholders. Because of his success in business he was appointed superintendent of purchases for the army in Massachusetts during the American Revolution, and this brought him a letter of commendation from General Washington.

In 1802 Phelps sold the Suffield house because of financial reverses.

Open: May 16 to October 15, daily, 1 to 5.

Admission: Nominal fee charged.

WALLINGFORD

NEHAMIAH ROYCE HOUSE: 538 S. Main Street.

This house, built in 1672, retains many of its original characteristics, such as the huge central chimney, gable-ended over-hang, and clapboarded sides. It is a sharp-peaked saltbox house, furnished with period pieces.

Its claim to fame lies in the fact that General Washington paused under the great elm here to bid good-bye to the people of Wallingford. He mentioned in his diary the mulberry trees, some of which are still standing.

Open: July and August, daily, 3 to 5.

Admission: Donation.

WETHERSFIELD

BUTTOLPH-WILLIAMS HOUSE: 240 Broad Street.

David Buttolph built this house in 1692, the year of his well-to-do father's death. It was a large house for the times—almost a mansion. He did not live in the house long since he moved from Wethersfield in 1698 to set up a tannery in Simsbury. Its next owner was Benjamin Beldon, who used it as a tavern. In 1721, Daniel Williams purchased it and his family retained possession of it for many years.

The house is a seventeenth-century frame house of Elizabethan design. The two-story structure is of post and girt construction and is sheathed with riven oak clapboards. There are heavy corner posts rising from the foundation to the second floor. It has two rooms on each floor, flanking a central chimney. The first floor contains a small entrance hall with a parlor to the left and a "hall," or kitchen, to the right. Two bedrooms are found on the second floor. The house has been restored to its original appearance and is furnished with period pieces.

"Ye Greate Kitchin," the heart of the household, has a completely equipped seventeenth-century kitchen. It contains early woodenware, furniture, and even a jack and weights listed in a 1692 inventory.

Open: May 15 to October 15, daily, 1 to 5.

Admission: Nominal fee charged.

JOSEPH WEBB HOUSE: 211 Main Street.

Joseph Webb built this house in 1752 when he was 25 years old; he lived in it with his wife, Mehitable Nott, for nine years. After his death, Mrs. Webb married Silas Deane, a great patriot who went to France to enlist the sympathies of the Marquis de Lafayette in the American cause. They moved out of the Webb House and went next door to the house that Deane had built, known today as the Silas Deane House. The original Webb House was later given to Joseph Webb, Jr., and his bride. The property acquired consisted of "dwelling house, barn, shop and all other buildings standing thereon."

The Webb House has its part in American history. In the spring of 1781, General George Washington and the Count de Rochambeau met here to make plans for a joint offensive against the English. The meeting marked the beginning of the Franco-American military alliance in actual field operations. The Yorktown campaign resulted in the surrender of Lord Cornwallis and the end of the American Revolution.

If Washington were to return to Wethersfield today, he would find Webb House very much as it was when he visited there in 1781, with only one change—the house is now white.

The room that attracts the most attention is the upstairs bedroom which still has the velvety, dark-red, flocked paper with a rich floral pattern on its walls, put up especially for the visit of George Washington. The south parlor, traditionally identified as the conference room, has been repaneled, and the house is beautifully furnished. Several items of furniture, silver, and china belonged to the Webb family.

Open: All year, Tuesday through Saturday 10 to 4, Sundays 1 to 4; closed Mondays all year and on Sundays from November 1 to April 20.

Admission: Nominal fee charged.

ISAAC STEVENS HOUSE: 215 Main Street.

This house was built in 1785 and is furnished with colonial antiques, including china, glassware, furniture, textiles, ladies' bonnets, and children's toys.

Open: Year round, Tuesday through Saturday, 10 to 4; May 15 to November 1, Sundays, 1 to 4.

Admission: Nominal fee charged.

SILAS DEANE HOUSE: Main Street.

Silas Deane, born in Groton, Connecticut, was graduated from Yale in 1758 and was admitted to the bar in 1761. He opened an office in Wethersfield and soon after married the widow of Joseph Webb. They had one son, Jesse, born in 1764.

Mrs. Deane died shortly after moving into the new house, which was built in 1766. Deane then married Elizabeth Saltonsall.

One of the military campaigns that helped inaugurate the American Revolution was planned in this house. It was also the headquarters for the Connecticut men who captured Fort Ticonderoga, a campaign to which Silas Deane contributed heavily. He was a member of the General Assembly of the New England states, and in 1774 went to Philadelphia as a delegate from Connecticut to the Continental Congress. In March, 1776, he was sent to France by Congress as a secret agent to induce the French government to lend financial assistance to Congress. In December, 1776, he was joined there by Benjamin Franklin and Arthur Lee. He remained abroad until 1789 and died aboard a ship in Deal Harbor, England, as he was about to return to America.

During the Revolution the mansion was the scene of much entertainment. Its outstanding architectural feature is its great double door.

Open: Year round, Tuesday through Saturday, 10 to 4; May 15 to November 1, also open Sundays, 1 to 4.

Admission: Nominal fee charged.

WINDSOR

Windsor is one of the oldest towns in the state, having been settled by William Holmes and a small company from Plymouth in 1633. In 1639, Windsor united with the towns of Hartford and Wethersfield under the "Fundamental orders" to form the colony of Connecticut.

ELLSWORTH HOMESTEAD: 778 Palisado Avenue.

This house was built in 1740 and was the home of Oliver Ellsworth, one of the five senators in the first Congress who made the first draft of the American Constitution. He was envoy to France after the Revolution and the third chief justice of the United States Supreme Court.

The house has a large central chimney and is furnished with antiques. It is said that Washington and John Adams were visitors here.

Open: May 1 to November 1, Tuesday through Saturday, 1 to 6.

Admission: Adults, nominal fee charged; children accompanied by adults, free.

FIRST CHURCH (CONGREGATIONAL): Palisado Avenue.
The present building was erected in 1794, but the organization is the oldest of its denomination in the New World. The adjoining burial ground contains Connecticut's oldest dated tombstone.
Open: Daily.
Admission: Free.

LT. WALTER FLYER HOMESTEAD: 96 Palisado Avenue.
Built in 1640, this is the oldest house in Windsor. It was a one-room house when Lieutenant Walter Flyer sold it to Captain Nathaniel Howard for 170 pounds sterling, but it soon began to grow. Every time the captain returned from a voyage, he would add a room. Mrs. Howard sold the fine silks and other foreign goods her husband brought back from the East. The side walls are filled with corncobs for insulation.
Open: Tuesday through Saturday, 10 to noon and 1 to 5; Sundays, 1 to 5; holidays by appointment; closed during January.
Admission: Adults, nominal fee charged; children accompanied by adults, free.

PALISADO GREEN
The Green occupies part of the site of the old stockade that was built here in 1637 during the Pequot War. It contains the Founders Monument, on which are listed the names of the settlers who came from England on the *Mary and John* in 1630.

WOODBURY

GLEBE HOUSE: Hollow Road.
This house was built in 1690 and enlarged in 1745. In 1783 during a secret meeting, Samuel Seabury, who lived in the house, was elected the first American bishop of the Episcopal Church. In 1784 he was consecrated in Aberdeen, Scotland.
The house is furnished in seventeenth- and eighteenth-century style.
Open: April 1 to October 31, Wednesday through Saturday 11 to 5, Sundays 1 to 5; November to April 1, Wednesday through Saturday 11 to 4; closed Tuesdays year round.
Admission: Donations.

Index

CONNECTICUT

MAINE

MASSACHUSETTS

NEW HAMPSHIRE

RHODE ISLAND

VERMONT

PHOTO CREDITS

Vermont Development Department, page 16; Shelburne Museum, Inc., pages 17 and 18; Preservation Society of Newport County, page 35; National Park Service, Department of Interior, page 54; Trustees of Preservations, Milton, Mass., page 59; Plymouth Chamber of Commerce, pages 79, 80, and 81; Plimoth Plantation, page 85; Old Sturbridge Village, pages 94 and 95; Connecticut Development Commission, pages 101, 102, and 107; Connecticut Historical Commission, page 109; New Canaan Historical Society, page 114; Antiquarian and Landmarks Society, page 116; Stamford Historical Society, page 119; Elinar Larson, page 119.

110   17